PUB STROLLS IN
DEVON

Michael Bennie

COUNTRYSIDE BOOKS
NEWBURY BERKSHIRE

COUNTRYSIDE BOOKS
3 Catherine Road
Newbury, Berkshire

To view our complete range of books,
please visit us at
www.countrysidebooks.co.uk

ISBN 1 85306 723 7

Photographs by the author
Designed by Graham Whiteman

Typeset by Techniset Typesetters, Newton-le-Willows
Produced through MRM Associates Ltd., Reading
Printed in Italy

Contents

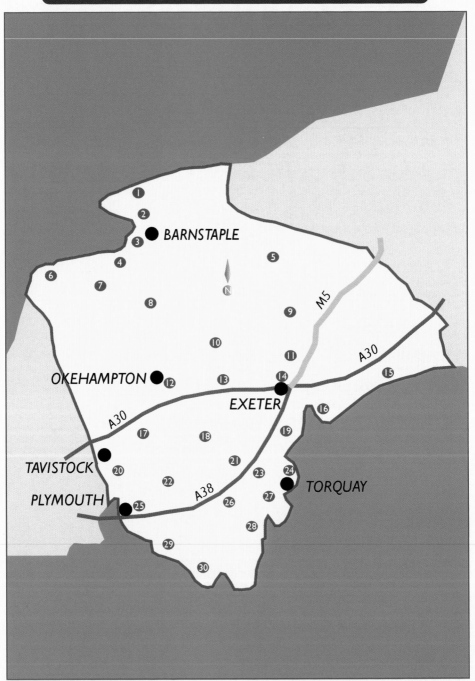

PUBLISHER'S NOTE

We hope that you obtain considerable enjoyment from this book; great care has been taken in its preparation. Although at the time of publication all routes followed public rights of way or permitted paths, diversion orders can be made and permissions withdrawn.

We cannot, of course, be held responsible for such diversion orders and any inaccuracies in the text which result from these or any other changes to the routes nor any damage which might result from walkers trespassing on private property. We are anxious though that all details covering the walks are kept up to date and would therefore welcome information from readers which would be relevant to future editions.

The simple sketch maps that accompany the walks in this book are based on notes made by the author whilst checking out the routes on the ground. However, for the benefit of a proper map, we do recommend that you purchase the relevant Ordnance Survey sheet covering your walk. The Ordnance Survey maps are widely available, especially through book-sellers and local newsagents.

Devon is perhaps as diverse a county as you are likely to find in England. Large cities and busy towns rub shoulders with stunning countryside, rugged coasts with undulating pastures, windswept moors with sheltered wooded valleys. Secluded villages and quiet lanes hide in the shadow of busy roads. It is also a county of rolling hills, with more than its fair share of stunning views. The county's pubs are equally varied, ranging from quiet village inns to busy city-centre hostelries, from cob and thatch to granite and slate, from the 14th to the 20th centuries.

The routes in this book reflect this variety, both of landscape and of hostelry. There is an amble through historic Plymouth and an exploration of the open spaces of Dartmoor, walks along farm and coastal paths, woodland and riverside rambles, a stroll around a beautifully preserved medieval and Tudor village, and much more. Many also visit places of particular interest – historic, cultural or scenic – along the way. Each route starts and finishes at or very near a pub that has been chosen for its character and the quality of its food and drink, including Dartmouth's 14th-century Cherub Inn, the converted farmhouse that is now the Grampus at Lee, the Prospect Inn on Exeter's Elizabethan quay and the 20th century Drum at Cockington, designed by the architect of New Delhi.

The walks are all suitable for family outings; none is longer than 4 miles and on most of them the terrain is generally easy. On the few occasions when there are hills or rough ground to negotiate, this is indicated in the route summary. The route descriptions and sketch maps should be self-explanatory, but if you want more detail, the relevant Ordnance Survey Landranger (1:25 000) and Explorer or Outdoor Leisure (1:50 000) maps are given. The former cover a larger area, but the latter have more detail, including field boundaries and so on. And if you are planning to make a day of it, each entry includes a few places of interest which are within easy reach.

The pub entries will hopefully give you a flavour of the atmosphere of the place, as well as an indication of the food and drink available and the opening hours. Bear in mind, however, that menus change, as do times of opening, so if you have any particular requirements or queries, a call to the phone number provided should confirm whether the information I have given is still valid. Where the pubs have their own car parks, the licensees are usually quite happy for customers to leave their cars there while walking, but please do ask before doing so.

Finally, I would like to thank Simon McCandlish, who accompanied me on many of these walks and whose stimulating company and occasional advice, particularly in the matter of photography, were much appreciated. The comment 'If I were you I would feel a photograph coming on about now' often alerted me to opportunities I would probably have missed had he not been with me.

Michael Bennie

Lee
The Grampus

MAPS: OS LANDRANGER 180 OR EXPLORER 139 (GR 483463)

WALK 1

DISTANCE: 3¾ MILES

DIRECTIONS TO START: LEE IS JUST WEST OF THE A361 ILFRACOMBE-BARNSTAPLE ROAD. IT IS SIGNPOSTED FROM THAT ROAD FROM THE ILFRACOMBE DIRECTION. IF YOU ARE COMING THE OTHER WAY, TURN LEFT ONTO THE B3343 WOOLACOMBE ROAD AND THEN FOLLOW THE SIGNS TO LEE. AT THE FIRST FORK IN THE VILLAGE CENTRE, GO LEFT TO REACH THE PUB. **PARKING:** IN THE PUB CAR PARK, WITH PERMISSION. ALTERNATIVELY, USE THE VILLAGE CAR PARKS.

Lee is a pretty village of colour-washed cottages stretching down a valley to the sea, with gracious Victorian houses on the hillsides above. Its peace and beauty belie its violent past, however, when this part of the Devon coast was the haunt of wreckers, who lured passing ships onto the treacherous rocks and pillaged their cargoes.

This varied route takes you up to the top of the cliffs above Lee, from where the wreckers would have shone their lights to confuse and mislead the ships' lookouts, and along the South West Coast Path, from where you get magnificent views. It then follows farm paths and tracks and returns to Lee down the beautifully wooded Borough Valley.

The Grampus

This attractive little pub is the oldest building in the village, although it has not been a pub for long. Its precise age is uncertain, but it was originally a farmhouse and was only converted to its present use in 1975. It retains its original thick slate walls, rendered and colour-washed on the outside but bare inside, and there is a large fireplace in the bar, today occupied by a wood-burning stove. Adjoining the bar is a small family and games room, and there is a pretty garden with an arbour.

The food is excellent and varied, using all fresh local produce. It ranges from the usual soups, sandwiches and ploughman's lunches to specials such as whitebait, balti dishes and steak and kidney pie. There are two real ales available in summer, but just one in winter. Also on tap are Whitbread Trophy, Murphy's stout, Stella Artois and Heineken lager and Blackthorn cider. The hours are 11 am to 3 pm and 6 pm to 11 pm in summer and 12 noon to 2.30 pm and 7 pm to 11 pm in winter, with the usual shorter Sunday opening. Telephone: 01271 862906.

The Walk

① Turn left as you leave the pub car park. After a short distance the lane narrows to a path and crosses a stream. It then runs alongside a field and emerges onto another lane. Follow that down to the sea, and at the T-junction turn left and follow the road as it climbs out of the village.

② About 250 yards from the junction you will see a Coast Path sign pointing right through a gate. Turn off here and follow the path up and along the cliffs. After several ups and downs you come out onto open heathland and soon you will see the Bull Point lighthouse down to your right. Skirt round to the left and you will come to a surfaced track leading away from the coast.

③ Turn left onto the track; as you do so, look half right for a good view of the puffin island of Lundy. After about $^1/_4$ mile you go through a gate and the track turns sharply to the right. Instead of following it round, go straight on along a footpath (signposted to Lee and Bennett's Mouth). It descends steeply into a valley; at the junction at the bottom, turn right (signposted to Mortehoe and Lee).

At the next junction, turn left across a footbridge (signposted to Lee). You climb to a gate, and eventually into a field. Keep to the right to reach a stile and turn right along the track on the other side. At the junction, follow the main track round to the right. You go through a gate and bear left, going through another two gates until you come to Damage Barton Farm.

④ Cross a stile and turn left, following the sign on the wall, which points to

Lee Bay

Warcombe Farm and Borough Wood. At the end, follow the track round to the left, and when you are faced with a gate, turn right along the less well-defined track. After a few yards turn left, following the yellow waymark, to a gate into a field. Turn right, and follow the path through the gorse. A waymarked post leads you to a gate.

Bear right along the next field to a fingerpost you can see on the near horizon. Turn left when you reach it and go down to a stile hidden among the bushes. Turn right on the other side to reach another stile leading to a lane. Cross the lane and another stile, and cross the next field, bearing slightly right. Cross yet another stile which leads you into Borough Wood.

⑤ Follow the path steeply down the hill, and at the bottom turn left (signposted to Lee). Cross another stile. After a little over $^1/_2$ mile you come out at yet another stile. Keep to the right of the field beyond to reach the last stile, which takes you onto the path you followed on the way out. Turn right to return to the Grampus.

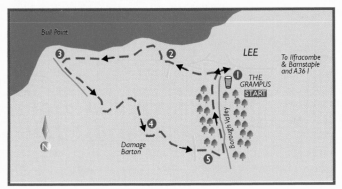

Georgeham
The Rock Inn

DIRECTIONS TO START: IF YOU ARE APPROACHING FROM THE SOUTH, TAKE THE B3231 FROM BRAUNTON TO CROYDE AND THEN CONTINUE ON TO GEORGEHAM; FROM THE NORTH, TAKE THE B3343 WEST OF THE A361 ILFRACOMBE-BARNSTAPLE ROAD AND TURN OFF LEFT, FOLLOWING THE SIGNS FOR GEORGEHAM. **PARKING:** THE PUB CAR PARK WITH PERMISSION OR IN VILLAGE SIDE STREETS.

Georgeham is a pretty village of whitewashed cottages and quiet lanes. Henry Williamson lived here for many years, and it was here that he wrote much of his classic *Tarka the Otter*. He is buried in the churchyard. The coast along here (large sections of which are featured in Williamson's book) is superb: long golden beaches punctuated by majestic cliffs.

Our walk takes us along a delightful lane, with some good views across the rolling hills, to the slopes above Woolacombe Sand. Another attractive lane brings us back to Georgeham through the picturesque hamlet of Putsborough, with more farmland views. It is all easy walking.

The Rock Inn

This charming 17th century pub has the low beams that are typical of the era. In addition to the main bar, it boasts a light, airy, plant-filled conservatory and a pleasant garden. It is open from 11 am to 3 pm and 6 pm to 11 pm during the week, but all day at weekends.

The food is all home cooked, and they pride themselves on using the best fresh produce. The menu ranges from jacket potatoes and the renowned Rock Inn rolls – 16 inch rolls with a variety of fillings – to fish, steak and pasta dishes. Another of the inn's claims to fame is that there is a choice of eight real ales; at the time of writing, the offerings included Greene King IPA, Cotleigh Golden Eagle, Abbot Ale, Young's Special and Wadworth 6X. Also on tap are Stella Artois, Budweiser, Foster's and Castlemaine lagers, Tetley's and Double Diamond bitter, Scrumpy Jack cider and Guinness. Telephone: 01271 890322.

The Walk

① Turn right and go down Rock Hill to the main road; turn left and follow the road for 100 yards until you come to a lane leading off to the right. Turn down it. As the lane curves to the left you pass Henry Williamson's house on your right. About 100 yards further on, turn right up a public footpath. It leads up between walls to a stile. Cross it and bear left across a field to another stile. Turn right in the next field and follow the boundary round to the left. Go through a gap in the

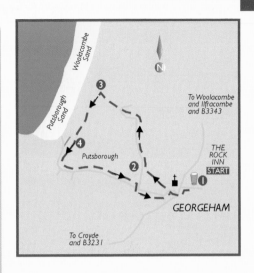

hedge and along the right-hand side of another field.

② At the end of the field you cross another stile into a lane; turn right. You continue to enjoy the view over the fields to the sea on your left as you follow this lane for 500 yards. When you come to Pickwell Manor Farm, follow the lane round to the right and then to the left past some cottages. At the junction, go right (signposted to Woolacombe and Ilfracombe). After a few yards turn left through a gate, following the public footpath sign. You go through another gate; keep to the left of the next field.

At the end of the field, bear left, keeping to the wall, and the whole stretch of Putsborough Sand comes into view. After a few yards turn half right, following the direction of the footpath sign (do not turn sharp right, otherwise you will find yourself on the wrong path). Make your way through the gorse and you will come out at a gate; carry on down the field beyond to another gate, hidden behind a bush.

The inviting sands at Putsborough

③ A few yards beyond the gate you come to the South West Coast Path; turn left. After $\frac{1}{4}$ mile or so, you will find a path leading off to the right; take it if you want to go down to the beach, and pick up the road at the end to rejoin the route.

④ The Coast Path comes out onto a track; go straight on, and when it joins a lane, go straight on again. You come to a junction; follow the main lane round to the left (signposted to Putsborough and Georgeham). Cross a ford alongside an ornamental pond and pass through the pretty hamlet of Putsborough. The lane climbs steadily but gently, and about $\frac{1}{2}$ mile beyond Putsborough you come to another junction, just beyond the village sign for Georgeham; carry straight on again. When you come to the village, ignore the side lanes and continue until you pass Williamson's house again. Follow the lane round to the right and at the T-junction turn left and after 100 yards right to return to the pub.

PLACES OF INTEREST NEARBY

At Croyde, about a mile to the west, you will find **Cascades**, a family adventure pool, and also a gem and mineral museum.

Fremington
The New Inn

DIRECTIONS TO START: FREMINGTON IS ON THE B3233 BETWEEN BARNSTAPLE AND INSTOW; THE PUB IS ON THE MAIN ROAD, TOWARDS THE EAST OF THE VILLAGE. **PARKING:** IN THE FREE PUBLIC CAR PARK ABOUT 100 YARDS FROM THE PUB TO THE EAST.

Henry Williamson's evocative wild-life story *Tarka the Otter* is set in North Devon, the 'Country of the Two Rivers' (the rivers being the Taw and the Torridge). The Tarka Trail is a long-distance route, some 180 miles long, which takes in most of the settings for Tarka's adventures – the lower Taw river, for example, is the scene of Tarka's 'Great Winter', and also where he and his mate caught a wild swan.

This easy amble takes in the part of the trail which runs alongside that stretch of river. A pretty, tree-lined path takes you to the trail, and a clear track brings you back to Fremington. The river is full of interest at all times; at low tide there are wading birds scouring the mudflats for food, and when the water is high there are fishermen on the shore and boats on the water.

The New Inn

This characterful old pub offers a warm welcome. It is long and narrow, with a cosy little bar just inside the main door and a larger, airy lounge further along the passage. The latter is beautifully decorated, and there are some delightful pictures and epigrams painted on the walls. There is also an attractive dining room on the right of the passage and a pretty little courtyard at the back.

The menu is wide-ranging, from sandwiches to steaks and roasts, with particularly fine fish. A range of drinks is also offered on draught. The cask ales are John Smith's, Bass and Wadworth 6X, and John Smith's Extra Smooth is available too, alongside Guinness, Stella Artois and Foster's lagers and Thatcher's Dry cider. Monday to Saturday hours are 11 am to 3 pm and 5.30 pm to 11 pm, with the usual Sunday opening. Telephone: 01271 373859.

The Walk

① Almost immediately across the main road from the pub, just a little to the left, you will see a public footpath sign. Follow it away from the road, between a stream and a wall. After a while the stream veers off to the right and you find yourself alongside a track instead. The path then swings left away from the track, and when it rejoins it, a few yards further on, it runs above it. You pass some houses and come out at Fremington Pill ('pill' is a local word for a creek). Follow the pill under some trees, cross a small footbridge and eventually, about $^1/_2$ mile after leaving

Fremington, you will go through a barrier and down to the dismantled railway that forms this stretch of the Tarka Trail.

② Bear right along the trail and cross a bridge over Fremington Pill. As you go, you get a very good view across the River Taw on your left. The trail becomes a road for a short stretch, and you pass Fremington station, now a café and cycle hire shop, on your right, with the old quay on your left. Towards the end of the stretch of road, take the track which bears slightly right to continue along the Tarka Trail.

③ After 600 yards, you will come to a bridge across the trail; turn left immediately before it and climb some steps to a track. Turn right and cross the bridge. Bear left on the other side, following the main track, and then after a few yards follow it round to the right. It passes a farm and some holiday cottages, and you get another pleasant view across the rolling hills ahead. You emerge onto a lane; turn left.

④ After 100 yards, just beyond a house called Little Meadows Cottage, you will

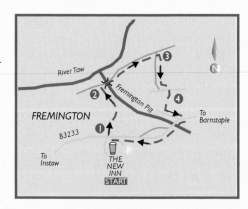

Fremington Pill at low tide

find a public footpath sign pointing down a green lane on the right; turn off here and follow the green lane into a field; keep to the left-hand boundary. You continue to get a good view across Fremington and the country beyond. Go through a gap in the hedge at the end and keep to the left of the next field. Cross a stile at the end into a lane; turn left. You are now alongside Fremington Pill again.

The lane comes out onto the B3233; turn right. As soon as you have crossed the pill, you will find a public bridleway sign pointing right. You can turn down here for a pretty, tree-lined diversion which cuts off a stretch of the road. It can become muddy after rain, however, so you may prefer to keep to the road. After $\frac{1}{4}$ mile the bridleway rejoins the road; bear right and you will find the pub on your left another $\frac{1}{4}$ mile further on.

PLACES OF INTEREST NEARBY

Barnstaple is 3 miles east of Fremington and here you will find an interesting **Heritage Centre**, as well as the **Museum of Barnstaple and North Devon**. A similar distance the other way, near Instow, is **Tapeley Park**, with its beautiful gardens.

Westleigh
The Westleigh Inn

| MAPS: OS LANDRANGER 180 OR EXPLORER 139 (GR 471287) | WALK 4 | DISTANCE: 4 MILES |

DIRECTIONS TO START: TAKE THE B3233 NORTH FROM THE A39 NEAR BIDEFORD AND FOLLOW IT ALONG THE EAST BANK OF THE RIVER TORRIDGE. AFTER ABOUT $^3/_4$ MILE YOU WILL SEE WESTLEIGH SIGNPOSTED TO THE RIGHT. IN THE VILLAGE TAKE THE FIRST TURNING ON THE LEFT AND THEN TURN LEFT AGAIN TO REACH THE PUB. **PARKING:** IN THE PUB CAR PARK BUT PLEASE ASK FIRST. THERE IS ALSO LIMITED PARKING IN THE VILLAGE.

Despite its proximity to a major road, Westleigh is a delightfully unspoilt little village overlooking the River Torridge. Along the riverbank below the village runs the Tarka Trail, a long-distance path which connects many of the places that feature in Henry Williamson's country classic, *Tarka the Otter*.

This route follows lovely lanes south from Westleigh, with some superb views both inland and out to sea. It then takes a quiet road down to the river, with another good view along the way, and joins the Tarka Trail (which here follows a disused railway line alongside the river) for the return to Westleigh. It is all easy walking on good surfaces.

The Westleigh Inn

This charming 15th century inn is tucked away in a forgotten corner of the village. It is full of character, with two cosy bars warmed by open fires in winter, a large beer garden with good views over the estuary of the Taw and the Torridge, and a children's play area.

There is a good selection of ales on tap – Bass, Ushers Best and Younger's Tavern are the regulars, but there are usually two guest beers on offer as well. In addition, you will find John Smith's Extra Smooth, Budweiser, Carlsberg, Foster's and Kronenbourg lagers, Black-thorn cider and Guinness. The food is delicious, and ranges from soups and jacket potatoes to steaks and a whole variety of other main courses. The home-made steak and Guinness pie is particularly recommended. Opening hours are 11.30 am to 3 pm and 6 pm to 11 pm Monday to Saturday, with the usual hours on Sunday. Telephone: 01271 860867.

PLACES OF INTEREST NEARBY

At **Tapeley Park Gardens**, about a mile north of Westleigh, you can see a wide range of garden habitats, from a walled kitchen garden to a tree-fringed lake, and from manicured lawns to the informality of a permaculture garden. There are also museums and other attractions at **Bideford** (1$\frac{1}{2}$ miles) and **Barnstaple** (6 miles).

The Walk

① Turn left and at the T-junction turn left again. You pass the church and leave the village. About 150 yards beyond the church you will see a public footpath sign pointing diagonally right across a stile. Follow it and cut across the corner of a field to another stile. Go diagonally right across the next field and look back as you do so for a lovely view across to the sea. When you get to the far corner, cross another stile and go down a track to a lane.

Turn left, and you get another very good view half right. At the junction about 150 yards down the lane, follow the main route round to the right (signposted to East-leigh). You go under the main road and swing to the left. After 500 yards you come to another junction; go right (signposted to Bideford). You climb a short hill, and when you reach the top, another good view opens up ahead and to the right.

② The lane ends at a road. Turn right and

To Instow

THE WESTLEIGH INN
START

River Torridge

B3233

WESTLEIGH

A39

To Bude

To Barnstaple

BIDEFORD

A386

②

③

To Torrington

The rather splendid Torridge Bridge

follow it for 1¼ miles. It is a quiet road, and broad enough for any cars that do come along to pass walkers without any problems. For most of this stretch you also get a grand view ahead across the river to Bideford. At the T-junction at the end, turn right.

③ At the next T-junction, at the main A386, turn left and then almost immediately right through a gap in a wall. Turn right on the other side along a broad track; this is the Tarka Trail. You go under the rather magnificent Torridge Bridge and a pleasant view opens up ahead along the estuary to Instow and beyond. After ¾ mile, when you are almost opposite a shipyard on the other side of the river, you will see a path going right to a bus shelter. Turn along it, and when you reach the road turn left. After a few yards you will come to the lane to Westleigh on your right. At the village, take the first turning on the left and then turn left again to reach the pub.

Molland
The London Inn

MAPS: OS LANDRANGER 181 OR OUTDOOR LEISURE 9 (GR 807283)

WALK 5

DISTANCE: 3¼ MILES

DIRECTIONS TO START: TAKE THE B3227 NORTH-EAST FROM THE A361 NORTH DEVON LINK ROAD NEAR SOUTH MOLTON, AND FOLLOW THE SIGNS TO MOLLAND. **PARKING:** THERE IS PUBLIC PARKING ALONGSIDE THE PUB, JUST BELOW THE CHURCH.

Exmoor National Park combines a spectacular coastline with open moors and rolling farmland and woods. Here, at its southern edge, it is the moor that predominates – wide open spaces, gentle, heather-covered slopes and a silence that can be felt. And the views from the high ground will take your breath away. Molland, a small village on the edge of the national park, complements the moor beautifully.

This route takes you up to Exmoor along a quiet lane, flower-fringed in summer, returning along farm tracks. The 15th century church, which you pass on your way out of the village, is worth a short detour, to see its old box pews and triple-decker pulpit, and once out in open country there is hardly a stretch in which the views are less than spectacular.

The London Inn

This gem of a pub is a 15th century coaching inn and retains many of its original features, including beamed ceilings, delightful inglenooks and wintertime log fires. It comprises a number of small, interconnecting rooms. One enters via a porch, which leads into an attractive lounge, to the left of which is the bar itself, and beyond that a cosy little family lounge. To the right of the main lounge is the spacious restaurant, furnished with lovely old pine tables. It is beautifully decorated throughout, with comfortable seats and sporting prints on the walls, and *definitely* no music or fruit machines. There is also a pleasant beer garden outside.

The pub is open from 11.30 am to 2.30 pm and 6 pm to 11 pm daily except Sunday, when it keeps the usual more restricted hours. The licensees alternate between the two local real ales, Exmoor and Cotleigh, and also have Worthington Best, Guinness, Stella Artois and Carlsberg lagers and Blackthorn cider on draught. The food is all home-made, from local produce as far as possible, and ranges from ploughman's lunches and jacket potatoes to steak and fish dishes. There is a separate evening menu. Telephone: 01769 550269.

The Walk

NB: A very short, simple stretch in the middle of the route is missing from the OS maps quoted above, Landranger 181 and Outdoor Leisure 9. It can be found on Landranger 180 and Explorer 127 respectively if needed.

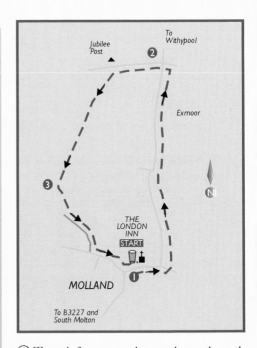

① Turn left as you leave the pub and follow the lane past the church (or turn up left to visit it). At the junction about 300 yards further on, follow the main lane round to the left (signposted to Sandyway, Hawkridge and Withypool). As you climb up towards the moor, you can look back over the farms and villages behind you for the first of the views. The lane is lined with hedges and flowers in season; the rosebay willowherb is particularly fine in summer. At the next junction, go straight on, and a little later cross a cattle-grid onto Exmoor proper. You now get an even better view back across the hills behind you; you can see the high ground of Dartmoor on a clear day. You also have a splendid view across the moor to your right, covered in a purple haze of heather in late summer.

② About ½ mile after crossing the cattle-grid, you come to a crossroads. Turn left

The view from Exmoor

(signposted to Twitchen). The view to the south remains with you as you follow this road for about $\frac{1}{4}$ mile to another cattle-grid. Just beyond is a large, weathered wooden post erected to commemorate the Queen's Silver Jubilee in 1977. Turn left across the open moor, following the bridlepath sign for Molland. There is a rough track, but you do not have to keep strictly to it – simply stay about 50 yards to the right of the fence. You can now enjoy the view uninterrupted, as it remains in front of you for most of the rest of the walk. You will come to a lane after about $\frac{1}{2}$ mile; cross it to a gate (there is a bridlepath sign for Molland, but it was broken when I last walked this route). Follow the track along the left-hand side of the field beyond.

③ Towards the end of the field you will find a gate on your left, marked with a blue waymark. Go through it and turn right along a track skirting the right-hand side of the field beyond, above a steep-sided valley. Go through a gate at the end onto another track. After 300 yards, go through another gate into a lane; turn left. At the first junction go straight on, and at the second, turn left (signposted to Hawkridge and Withypool), and you will find the pub on your left just beyond the village stores.

PLACES OF INTEREST NEARBY

At South Molton, 6 miles south-west of Molland, is **Quince Honey Farm**, which has exhibitions of bee-keeping and honey-making, and just beyond, at Clapworthy Mill, is **Hancock's Devon Cider**, where you can see cider being made.

Hartland
The Hart Inn

DIRECTIONS TO START: THE B3248 RUNS THROUGH HARTLAND IN A CIRCUIT FROM THE A39 BIDEFORD-BUDE ROAD. THE HART INN IS JUST OFF THE SQUARE, IN THE CENTRE OF THE VILLAGE NEXT TO THE PUBLIC CAR PARK. **PARKING:** USE THE FREE PUBLIC CAR PARK ALONGSIDE THE PUB, WHICH IS SIGNPOSTED FROM THE MAIN STREET.

In Elizabethan times, Hartland was a major centre – more important even than Bideford – served by its own harbour at Hartland Quay to the west, but it is now a quiet, attractive backwater.

Our route takes us through Hartland and down to the valley of the Abbey River. It passes Hartland Abbey and then turns south, running through the neighbouring hamlet of Stoke, with its imposing church dedicated to St Nectan, a Welsh missionary who was martyred here in the 6th century. The final leg follows lanes and tracks back to Hartland. There are a few lovely woodland stretches and some superb views, and although you have to climb to enjoy the latter, the hills are not unduly steep.

The Hart Inn

This is an unusual old pub; as one enters, one is faced by a stone passageway, with the bar on the left and two snug little rooms, interestingly called Cobblers and The Shop, on the right. At the end is a small, open courtyard, with a door leading out to the garden at the back.

With its interesting layout, bare stone walls and low ceilings, this is a pub full of character. There is an open fireplace in the bar, and the other rooms are both cosy places to enjoy a meal or a drink. The food is very varied, ranging from soups, pasta snacks and jacket potatoes to main courses such as chicken balti, chilli and different steak dishes. The drinks are equally varied: on tap there are Webster's, Flowers IPA, Courage Directors, Best and Mild, John Smith's Extra Smooth, Foster's, Heineken, Guinness and Blackthorn cider. Opening hours are 12 noon to 3 pm and 6 pm to 11 pm on Monday to Thursday, and all day on Friday, Saturday and Sunday. Telephone: 01237 441474.

The Walk

① On leaving the pub, turn right and follow the road out of the village. As it swings to the left, just before the derestriction sign, turn right down a surfaced track, following the public footpath sign. When you get to the gate into the observatory at the end, turn left through a kissing-gate and along the path on the other side. Follow it to the right at the end, round the observatory grounds, and then left through a gap in a bank, into a wood.

The 'lonely' stile with Stoke church behind

It becomes a broad track as it runs downhill through the wood; at the bottom it swings right and you cross the Abbey River via a footbridge. Go diagonally left across a field to a stile leading onto another track. At the fork, go right along

PLACES OF INTEREST NEARBY

Hartland Abbey, which you pass along the way, is open at certain times during the summer. Also nearby, just 600 yards off this route and a mile south of Stoke, is **Docton Mill and Gardens**, a watermill with a beautiful garden open to the public.

a path which climbs up through another lovely wood. After a few hundred yards it leaves the wood via a stile and runs along the right-hand edge of a field.

②At the end of the field, cross another stile onto a track; turn left. Follow this track for 500 yards or so, into the wood again. At the junction, ignore the turning going off sharp left and follow the main track for a few more yards down to a lane. Turn right, passing the gate to Hartland Abbey, and follow the lane as it swings left and then right. It swings right again, and 100 yards after it does so you will see a public footpath sign pointing left into a field. Follow it through a gate and bear right.

You will see a rather incongruous stile standing alone in the middle of the field, with no sign of a fence on either side. Pass it and cross another stile at the end of the field (this time in a fence). Keep to the right of the next field, and in the far corner cross two stiles in quick succession, with steps in between. Keep to the right of the next field to a gate leading into a lane; turn left and follow the lane down a

hill. At the bottom you will see Hartland Abbey on the left. The lane swings left across a bridge and winds and climbs up the other side to Stoke.

③At the junction by the church, turn left. After a few yards turn right up another lane. At the crossroads 150 yards up the lane, go straight on along a track. As you come over the brow of the hill, you get another good view up ahead of you. The track deteriorates as it winds down to cross a stream and then climbs up on the other side. At the top, at Wargery Farm, you join a lane; turn right.

④At the crossroads turn left (signposted to Stoke and Hartland). At the junction after 500 yards go left (signposted to Stoke and Hartland Quay). At the next junction go left and immediately right. This lane takes you down to cross another stream. As it begins to climb up the other side of the valley, turn left up a green lane (signposted to Hartland).

When the green lane turns left through a gate, go straight on across a stile into a wood. Follow the path through the wood to a track across a field at the bottom. At the end of the field, follow the track up through a wood to a stile. Follow the path on the other side to a gate, which leads into a road; turn right. At the junction turn left and then right to return to the pub and the car park.

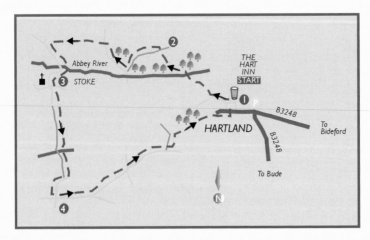

Parkham
The Bell Inn

MAPS: OS LANDRANGER 190 OR EXPLORER 126 (GR 387211)

WALK 7

DISTANCE: 3$\frac{1}{2}$ MILES

DIRECTIONS TO START: PARKHAM IS ABOUT 1$\frac{1}{2}$ MILES SOUTH OF THE A39 BIDEFORD-BUDE ROAD, AND IS SIGNPOSTED. THE PUB IS ON THE SOUTHERN EDGE OF THE VILLAGE ON THE ROAD TO BUCKLAND BREWER. **PARKING:** CUSTOMERS ARE WELCOME TO LEAVE THEIR CARS IN THE PUB CAR PARK, WITH PERMISSION. THERE IS ALSO PARKING IN THE ROAD.

This is a lovely, unspoilt part of North Devon, an area of gentle hills, green fields, quiet lanes and pretty villages. This attractive, easy ramble takes you from one such village along lanes lined with flowers in summer and past hedgerows filled with wildlife to the cool greenery of North Melbury Plantation and back again. There are some excellent views as you go, with woods and farms stretching away in all directions, and the Bristol Channel visible in the distance on a clear day.

The Bell Inn

Converted from three 14th-century cottages and the village forge, the Bell is a delightful pub, which oozes character. It has low beams and exposed stone walls (even the bar counter is built of stone) and its open fire and two wood-burning stoves give it a warm, friendly atmosphere on cold days, which is matched by the welcome accorded to visitors all year round. There is a large bar with some snug nooks, a separate pool room and a most attractive non-smoking dining area in the old forge at the back.

All the food is home-made, and ranges from a number of fish and steak dishes to specials such as beef stroganoff and chicken in orange and apricot, as well as the usual snacks. The regular cask ales are Bass and Exmoor, and these are supplemented by guest ales. Also on tap are Worthington Creamflow, Caffrey's, Carling and Grolsch lager, Scrumpy Jack cider and Guinness. Monday to Saturday opening times are 12 noon to 2 pm and 6.30 pm to 11 pm, with shorter hours on Sundays. Telephone: 01237 451201.

The Walk

NB: Stout shoes or boots are advisable after rain as one or two places in the plantation (point 2) can become a little wet – but it is usually possible to walk round any muddy patches.

① Turn right as you leave the pub and cross to Melbury Road, alongside the school. This lane soon takes you out of the village behind high banks full of wild

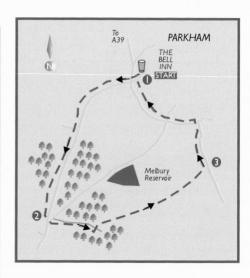

flowers in season and topped by attractive hedgerows. After about $\frac{1}{2}$ mile you come to a junction; go straight on. You pass a conifer plantation, and as you leave it you get a good view across to the right.

② The lane joins a more major road at a T-junction; cross the road and follow the public bridleway sign on the other side along a broad track into North Melbury Plantation. After $\frac{1}{4}$ mile you will see another public bridleway sign pointing off the track to the left. Turn off here and follow a path, which starts off fairly narrow but soon broadens as it leads you deeper into the plantation. When you come to a junction, with a clear track going off to the left, ignore it and follow the less clear path straight ahead.

After $\frac{1}{2}$ mile you emerge into a cleared area and get a superb view to your left, across Melbury Reservoir and the rolling hills beyond. You also get a good view across the bank on your right. At the end you go through a gate into a field; keep to the right to reach a gate at the end and

Melbury Reservoir from North Melbury Plantation

keep to the right again in the next field. You can still enjoy the beautiful view to your left. Go through a gap in the hedge at the end and cross one more field to a gate leading into a lane.

③ Turn left and follow the lane for about 600 yards to a T-junction; turn left (signposted to Parkham). This lane winds down to cross a stream and comes out at a crossroads; go straight on (signposted to Parkham again). After 700 yards you will find yourself back at the

crossroads on the edge of the village, with the pub on the right.

PLACES OF INTEREST NEARBY

Clovelly, a beautifully preserved and privately owned fishing village, is about 6 miles away. On the way to it, you pass **The Milky Way and North Devon Bird of Prey Centre**, which combines the attractions of a farm park with slides, rides and a falconry display. About 4 miles in the other direction, towards Bideford, is **The Big Sheep**, another farm park, with sheep racing, shows and displays.

Great Torrington
The Black Horse

| **MAPS:** OS LANDRANGER 180 OR EXPLORER 126 (GR 495191) | **WALK 8** | **DISTANCE:** 2¹⁄₂ MILES |

DIRECTIONS TO START: GREAT TORRINGTON IS ABOUT 9 MILES SOUTH OF BIDEFORD ON THE A386 OKEHAMPTON ROAD. THE BLACK HORSE IS IN HIGH STREET, IN THE CENTRE OF THE TOWN.
PARKING: THE SMALLER OF THE TWO LONG-STAY CAR PARKS, AT THE END OF CASTLE STREET (SEE END OF POINT 4). IF THAT IS FULL, TRY THE LARGER CASTLE HILL CAR PARK, OFF SOUTH STREET.

Great Torrington (or simply 'Torrington' as it is usually called) is a pretty market town sitting high above the River Torridge and commanding superb views of the surrounding countryside. The High Street, the pannier market and the area around the church are particularly attractive. Its main historical claim to fame is as the site of the last major battle of the English Civil War, when the Roundheads and Cavaliers, 15,000 men in all, fought their way through its streets and barricades in February 1646.

To the north, west and south of the town lies the Great Torrington Common, a delightful public open space criss-crossed with paths. This walk explores the southern section, avoiding streets and roads and taking you along the peaceful banks of the Torridge and up the beautifully wooded hillside above it.

The Black Horse

Like Torrington itself, the Black Horse also has a Civil War history. It is said to have been the headquarters of both the leader of the Royalists, Lord Hopton, and – after he was ousted – the Parliamentary general, Sir Thomas Fairfax. It was old even before then, however – parts of the building are believed to date from the 11th century.

It is a charming inn, set right on the street, with a small bar to one side of the door and an attractive family room on the other. At the back is a large restaurant with an enormous fireplace, which now holds a wood-burning stove.

It is open at the normal times during the week and on Sundays, but all day on Saturdays. There is a good range of bar snacks and main meals, ranging from steak to vegetarian dishes. Fish is a particular speciality. On tap they have Courage Directors and Best, John Smith's Cask and Extra Smooth, Foster's, Carlsberg and Kronenbourg lagers, Guinness and Dry Blackthorn cider. There is also a guest ale which changes regularly. Telephone: 01805 622121.

The Monument, Great Torrington

The Walk

① As you leave the pub, turn right. At the end of High Street, after a few yards, turn right again into South Street, and follow it until you come to a junction, where the main route turns right. Go straight on into Mill Street, but instead of following it down the hill take the path that leads straight on into Rack Park. At the other end of the park join a road and continue straight on.

② After about 200 yards, just before the road curves to the right, you will see a surfaced footpath going left down the hill; take that. It takes you across a stretch of the common, with good views over the River Torridge. As you get towards the bottom of the hill you cross another surfaced path; carry straight on onto an unsurfaced grassy path. This emerges at a road; cross over to a track which leads you into a stretch of trees and bracken. It bears right and crosses another track; go straight across onto a short surfaced stretch, past a water treatment works.

③ Just beyond the water treatment works you will come to the river; turn left to cross a stile. Keep to the right of the field beyond, alongside the river. Cross another stile and keep to the right of the next field. You pass a factory on your left and cross a fence via some concrete steps. There is an abundance of wild flowers along here in summer.

You emerge onto a road at Taddiport Bridge; turn left and almost immediately right down a small road, which soon becomes a track. There is a public footpath sign, but it is a little way along and not easily visible from the main road. The track narrows to a path and goes up to cross another track; bear right along the track and follow it. There is a wealth of summer flowers again along here (foxgloves in particular), and the steep hillside on your left is covered in trees, gorse and bracken.

④ Just over ½ mile after crossing the road, as the river bends to the right, you will see a track leading off to the left into the trees; follow it up to some steps, and at the top of the steps turn left. After a few yards you have a choice of three paths; take the middle, surfaced, one. You will come to a stone obelisk, a monument erected by the women of Torrington to the men who fell at the Battle of Waterloo; turn right and you will pass a stone indicating that this is called George's Path. The views from here are quite stunning.

Ignore the paths leading off to right and left, and keep to the surfaced path. You will emerge at an open space with picnic tables next to the car park. Turn right, and to return to the pub, go through the car park and then through the very attractive, bustling pannier market. This brings you out just opposite High Street.

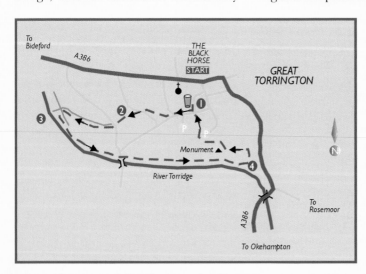

Halberton
The Barge

MAPS: OS LANDRANGER 181 OR EXPLORER 128 (START AND FINISH) AND 114 (MIDDLE) (GR 013128)

WALK 9

DISTANCE: 3$\frac{1}{2}$ MILES

DIRECTIONS TO START: HALBERTON IS JUST SOUTH OF THE A361 BETWEEN TIVERTON AND THE M5 AND ABOUT 3 MILES FROM EACH. THE BARGE IS AT THE EASTERN END OF THE VILLAGE. **PARKING:** IN THE PUB CAR PARK, BUT PLEASE ASK FIRST. OTHERWISE THERE IS LIMITED PARKING IN SOME OF THE SIDE ROADS OFF THE MAIN ROAD THROUGH THE VILLAGE. ALTERNATIVELY, YOU CAN PARK IN THE CAR PARK ON THE BANK OF THE GRAND WESTERN CANAL ALONGSIDE THE HALBERTON-TIVERTON ROAD TO THE WEST OF THE VILLAGE AND START THE WALK AT POINT 3.

Halberton is a pretty village tucked into a bend in the Grand Western Canal, with a lovely duckpond and a very attractive church. This easy route explores its back lanes before heading out to the canal. It then follows the towpath as it meanders through rolling farmland before returning to the pub along a farm track

It is a lovely walk in any season, but my favourite time is early summer, when the banks are ablaze with wild flowers, the canal itself is fringed with water lilies and there are usually a few ducklings, cygnets and coot chicks to be seen on the water.

31

The Barge

Built in the early 19th century, this is an attractive, welcoming pub, with a lot of character. It is unusual in that one end of the main lounge is carpeted and furnished with deep armchairs and a settee, while the other end has bare wooden floors with the more usual tables and chairs. Behind the lounge is a comfortable non-smoking dining area and at the back is what they call the Sports Bar, with TV, a pool table and a skittle alley. The overall impression is light and airy, although there are warming fires in winter. There is also a beer garden to the rear of the pub.

Traditional pub food is served, all home-made and ranging from snacks to main courses and a tempting array of desserts. Bass is on tap, as well as John Smith's, Worthington Creamflow and Draught, Tennent's Pilsner, Foster's and Grolsch lager, Guinness and Blackthorn cider. The Barge is open from 12 noon to 3 pm and from 5 pm to 11 pm on Monday to Saturday, and all day on Sundays. Telephone: 01884 820316.

The Walk

① Follow the main road into the village. After about 500 yards, you will see the post office on your right, with a little lane called Pond Hill on your left. Go down it and pass the pretty pond on the right. The lane narrows as it passes between two attractive whitewashed cottages, and on the other side it becomes a path. Follow the path to the left, and at the junction at the corner of the churchyard turn right. At the far end

PLACES OF INTEREST NEARBY

The **museum at Tiverton**, 3 miles west of Halberton, is one of the largest social history museums in the South West and traces the history of the area since Roman times. Just north of Tiverton is **Knightshayes Court**, a Victorian house and garden owned by the National Trust.

of the churchyard the path goes to the left and becomes a road again, passing the village school.

② At the T-junction, turn left. Ignore the side roads, just keep to the road you are on for about $1/4$ mile until you see a lane called Crownhill on your right. Turn off here and follow the lane out of the village. About 600 yards after joining it, you will come to a group of houses and a bridge over the Grand Western Canal. Turn right through a gate just before it, to join the canal towpath.

③ After about 300 yards you pass under a bridge, and you will find parking areas on both sides of the canal. The canal swings sharply to the left, and as you follow it you get a good view across the surrounding countryside. The bankside is filled with wild flowers in summer, and there are usually herons, ducks, swans and coots to be seen. After a few hundred yards the canal bends to the right and you enter a small wood.

On the other side of the wood, the canal swings right again and then straightens out somewhat. You pass under another bridge, and you can see Halberton and its church half right across the fields. After 600 yards you go under another bridge and then, $1/4$ mile beyond,

The Grand Western Canal

go up the bank to the right to leave the towpath via a gate.

④ You come out on a track; go straight on and follow the track round to the right after 100 yards or so. It emerges onto the main road through Halberton; turn right and you will find the pub on your left after 100 yards.

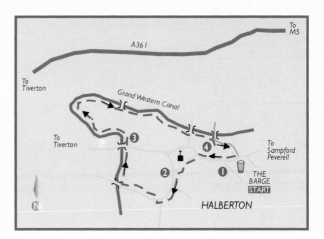

Morchard Bishop
The London Inn

MAPS: OS LANDRANGER 191 OR EXPLORER 113 (GR 770074)

WALK 10

DISTANCE: $3^3/_4$ MILES

DIRECTIONS TO START: THE VILLAGE IS ABOUT 2 MILES OFF THE A377 CREDITON-BARNSTAPLE ROAD AND IS CLEARLY SIGNPOSTED. THE LONDON INN IS IN THE CENTRE OF THE VILLAGE. **PARKING:** IN THE PUB CAR PARK, BUT PLEASE ASK FIRST. THERE IS ALSO A FREE PUBLIC CAR PARK IN CHURCH STREET.

Morchard Bishop is a pleasant mixture of the old and the new: cob and thatch cottages rub shoulders with rendered, slate-roofed houses and modern bungalows. It boasts what is reputed to be the longest row of thatched cottages in England – a pretty chain of traditional houses set back from Fore Street just below the pub.

It is ideal walking country; indeed the village lies virtually in the middle of the Two Moors Way, a long-distance path that runs from Ivybridge, on the southern edge of Dartmoor, to Lynmouth on the Exmoor coast. Our route follows part of the trail before diverting onto a farm path and returning along a delightful green lane. It is easy walking, and the views along the way are superb.

The London Inn

The inside of this 16th-century coaching inn belies its somewhat stark exterior: it is in fact a warm and welcoming place, full of character. Although the bar is roomy, the bare stone walls, black beams, wood-burning stove and plushly upholstered furniture all combine to give it a snug, comfortable air. And if you are visiting it in summer, you will enjoy the garden at the back.

All the food is good, home-cooked fare, ranging from snacks and salads to specials like steak and ale pie and roasts. They pride themselves on their servings – what the landlady calls 'farmers' portions' – so it is probably best to call in for a meal *after* your walk rather than before! The draught offerings when I last called were London Pride, Sharp's Cornish Coaster, Boddingtons, Whitbread Best, Heineken, Stella Artois, Foster's and Guinness, but the ales are subject to change from time to time. Opening times Monday to Saturday are 12 noon to 3 pm and 6.30 pm to 11.30 pm, apart from Monday lunchtime when the inn is closed. On Sunday, the normal opening hours apply. Telephone: 01363 877222.

The Walk

NB: After rain there may be muddy patches on the return leg of the walk – stout shoes or boots are recommended.

① Turn right as you leave the pub and after a few yards left up a track, following the Two Moors Way sign. After a short distance it ends at a house; cross a stile on the left and then go through a kissing-

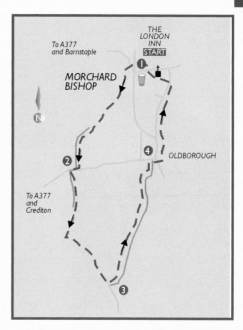

gate. Bear right across the field on the other side to another kissing-gate and then bear left in the next field to two gates. Go through the right-hand one, which is marked with the Two Moors Way waymark, and along the left-hand side of a field to a stile. Keep to the left of the next field to a track; go straight on to another stile alongside a gate.

Keep to the left again on the other side. As you go down the field you get a lovely view across the undulating hills ahead of you, all the way to Dartmoor. At the bottom of the field go through a gate onto a track and turn left. At the end go through another gate and bear right to a stile. Go straight across the next field. A gate leads you into a green lane. Go through another gate and follow the green lane on the other side past a couple of houses until it joins a road.

② Turn right and after a few yards left along a drive, following the Two Moors

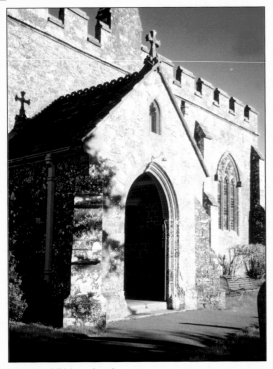

Morchard Bishop church

with it on your left. Follow it round to the left, to the right and then to the left again. Pass some farm buildings to reach a junction, with a lane on the right and a track running straight on.

③ Go up the track, which is marked with a public bridleway sign. After about 500 yards you pass a house called Gollands and the track becomes a narrower green lane, fringed with attractive hedgerows. This is where the going can become a bit muddy and wet after rain, but it is quite passable. It swings to the right and then to the left, narrowing as it does so.

④ About ³/₄ mile after passing Gollands, you emerge, past a house, onto a lane at the hamlet of Oldborough. Turn right and then immediately left (signposted to Morchard Bishop). After 300 yards you will come to a lane going off to the right; take it. After another 600 yards you come to another junction; go straight on. About 150 yards beyond this junction there is a public footpath leading through a gate on the left; follow it across a small field and through another gate into the churchyard. Follow the path round to the left of the church and out into a road; turn left and after 250 yards, at the junction, turn left to the London Inn.

Way waymark and public footpath sign. This leads to another green lane, and you get another good view up ahead. At the end, go through a gate and along the right-hand edge of a field. At the end of the field, cross a stream and then a stile, and turn right along the edge of a stand of small trees.

Go through a gap in the hedge at the end and leave the Two Moors Way by turning left up a track past a house. Follow the track through a gate into a field and go diagonally right to a stile in the far corner. As you cross the field, Dartmoor again comes into view half right. Keep to the right of the next field until you come to a gap in the hedge on your right; go through and continue along the hedge, but now

---

PLACES OF INTEREST NEARBY

Three miles to the south-west of Morchard Bishop, on the other side of the A377, is the **Down St Mary Vineyard and Winery**, where you can tour the vineyards and taste the wine.

Stoke Canon
The Stoke Canon Inn

MAPS: OS LANDRANGER 192 OR EXPLORER 114 (GR 938979)

WALK 11

DISTANCE: 2½ MILES

DIRECTIONS TO START: THE A396 EXETER-TIVERTON ROAD GOES THROUGH STOKE CANON AND THE PUB IS ON THE MAIN ROAD. **PARKING:** THE LICENSEES HAVE NO OBJECTION TO CUSTOMERS LEAVING THEIR CARS IN THE PUB CAR PARK WHILE THEY WALK, BUT PLEASE ASK FIRST. OTHERWISE THERE IS PARKING IN THE ROAD OUTSIDE.

The Exe Valley Way is a long-distance path which, as its name suggests, follows the valley of the River Exe all the way from below Exeter to Exebridge, on the Somerset border. This tranquil country amble covers a particularly attractive stretch of the route, where the Exe glides silently through fields and meadows between overhanging trees and banks filled with wild flowers.

Starting in the attractive village of Stoke Canon, quiet lanes take you to the river. Field paths follow the riverbank to skirt the neighbouring village of Brampford Speke before you turn back along a dismantled railway line fringed with trees. There are some beautiful views to enjoy along the way, and because the route is mainly across the river's flood plains, it is all flat and easy walking.

The Stoke Canon Inn

Built some 300 years ago, this is an attractive little pub, where visitors receive a real Devon welcome. The original stone walls have been exposed in places, giving it a warm, cosy atmosphere. There are three sections: the main bar, a games area to the side and a light, airy room towards the back. All are comfortably furnished and carpeted. There is also a beer garden at the back, with a children's play area.

The pub opens at 11.30 am on Monday to Saturday and 12 noon on Sundays. It closes during the afternoon on weekdays, but is open all day at weekends. There is a good variety of home-made food available, ranging from sandwiches to lasagne and steak and ale pie. The 'resident' ales are Bass and Tetley's, and there is always a local guest ale available. Other draught offerings include Whitbread Trophy, Stella Artois and Carling lagers, Blackthorn cider, Guinness and Murphy's. Telephone: 01392 841200.

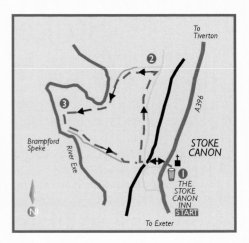

The Walk

① Cross the main road to Chestnut Crescent and follow that until it turns to the left. When it does, go straight on across a railway line and follow the road round to the right. Pass Oakhay Barton on your left and continue along the pretty lane. As you do so, you get a good view ahead of the patchwork of fields and hedges.

② A little over ¹/₂ mile after crossing the railway line, you will come to a lane going off to the left, with a cross marking the junction. Turn left here. You pass some Victorian cottages and the lane becomes a track. About 200 yards further on, the track forks; go left to a gate into a field. Keep to the right of the field on the other side, alongside the river. The banks along here are a mass of Himalayan balsam in late summer.

Cross a double stile at the end of the field and keep to the right of the next one, still following the river. Cross another double stile and go straight across the next field, while the river curves away to the right. You come to a rough track, which leads you to a gate. Follow the left-hand boundary of the field beyond to reach another two gates.

③ Turn left after the second gate and keep to the left of the field beyond until you come to a footbridge on your left.

PLACES OF INTEREST NEARBY

Three miles north-east of Stoke Canon is the National Trust property of **Killerton House**. About 4 miles to the south is **Exeter**, with its cathedral, museums and other attractions.

The River Exe

Cross it and bear right to a kissing-gate and a path, which leads you up to the embankment along which the now dismantled railway used to run. The path is lined with tall trees along here, but you soon emerge to find yourself alongside the river again.

Go through a kissing-gate and continue along the embankment until you meet a fence. Bear left through another kissing-gate and cross a field to a third. Follow the path beyond between fences to a final kissing-gate which brings you out onto the road by the level crossing. Cross the railway line and follow Chestnut Crescent back to the pub.

Sticklepath
The Devonshire Inn

MAPS: OS LANDRANGER 191, EXPLORER 113, OR OUTDOOR LEISURE 28 (GR 641940)

WALK 12

DISTANCE: $1\frac{3}{4}$ MILES

DIRECTIONS TO START: TURN OFF THE A30 AT THE OKEHAMPTON TURNING AND FOLLOW THE SIGNS FIRST FOR BELSTONE AND THEN FOR STICKLEPATH. **PARKING:** THE PUB CAR PARK IS ACROSS THE ROAD FROM THE DEVONSHIRE INN ITSELF, AND THE LANDLORD HAS NO OBJECTON TO CUSTOMERS LEAVING THEIR CARS THERE WHILE THEY WALK (BUT PLEASE ASK BEFORE YOU DO SO). THERE IS ALSO PARKING IN THE STREET OUTSIDE AND AT FINCH FOUNDRY NEXT DOOR.

The River Taw, which rises high on Dartmoor and flows through Sticklepath on its way to the sea at Barnstaple, was the location for much of the action in Henry Williamson's classic tale, *Tarka the Otter*. Part of our route passes through the lovely Skaigh Wood to the west of the village, where Tarka fought for a rabbit with a group of stoats.

Indeed, this route crams a lot of variety into a relatively short distance. There is the attractive village of Sticklepath to explore at the start, followed by superb views over Dartmoor as you follow quiet farm tracks above the valley, then a delightful wooded stretch along the riverbank, and the chance to visit a working water-powered forge at the end.

The Devonshire Inn

Originally a row of Elizabethan cottages, one of which was granted an ale and cider licence some 300 years ago, this attractive, old-fashioned pub has remained essentially a local watering hole, eschewing many of the 'improvements' that others have introduced to attract the passing trade. It comprises three rooms, all half-panelled, but each with its own character. The main bar has a tiled floor and is furnished with the usual tables, chairs and stools. Next door is a carpeted lounge with armchairs and occasional tables containing a variety of magazines. And across the way from the entrance is a small games room, also tiled and with tables and chairs. At the back is a pretty beer garden.

The pub is open all day, and offers three cask-conditioned ales: Bass, Tinners and Hicks Special Draught. Also on tap are Carlsberg lager, Young's Oatmeal Stout and Luscombe cider. The food is delicious, but restricted at lunchtimes to ploughman's lunches, pasties and sandwiches. Meals are available in the evenings by special order. Telephone: 01837 840626.

The Walk

① Turn left outside the pub and follow the road out of Sticklepath. At the edge of the village, turn left along a lane (signposted to Skaigh) and immediately right up a track, following the bridlepath sign for Tongue End and Skaigh. There is a fairly stiff climb at first, but only for about 200 yards or so. The rosebay

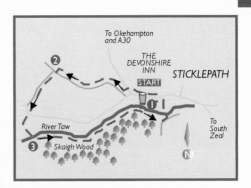

willowherb is particularly fine along here in summer.

When you come to a house, follow the track to the left. Before you do so, however, look to the right for a good view of this northern fringe of Dartmoor across the fields. Once you have turned, the track narrows to a path and becomes less steep, soon levelling off completely. From time to time you get another fine view through gateways to the tors of Dartmoor. You go through a gate and follow the track on the other side.

② About 50 yards beyond the gate, you will see another track leading off left, signposted to Skaigh. Follow it for $1/4$ mile to some houses and a lane. Go straight on down the lane and when it swings left, go straight on again, along a path into a pretty wood. Follow it round to the right and down a steep hill. At the bottom you come to a track; turn left and after a few yards right along another footpath. Bear left through the trees to the River Taw.

③ You cross a footbridge; notice the quote from *Tarka the Otter* carved on the railings. Go through the gate on the other side and follow the path alongside the river. This is a delightful stretch, with the river splashing over the rocks and cascades

The summer-house at Finch Foundry

alongside you and the cool woods above. This whole area is a mass of rhododendrons. After about 600 yards you cross a stile and continue alongside the river.

You eventually come out at a track; turn left, following the sign to Sticklepath. Go through a gate and a short distance further on turn left across another footbridge (signposted to the Museum of Water Power). Follow the path on the other side alongside a small stream. It passes a Quaker burial ground and emerges at the back of Finch Foundry. You can go through

the car park on the left to return to the pub through its beer garden, or bear right to visit the Foundry or go through an archway to the main street.

> ## PLACES OF INTEREST NEARBY
> The National Trust property of **Finch Foundry**, which you pass at the end of the walk, is a 19th-century water-powered forge, which is still in operation. At **Okehampton**, 3 miles away, you can visit the Norman **castle**, now owned by English Heritage, and the **Museum of Dartmoor Life**.

Tedburn St Mary
The King's Arms Inn

MAPS: OS LANDRANGER 191 OR EXPLORER 114 (GR 814941)

WALK 13

DISTANCE: 3 MILES

DIRECTIONS TO START: TEDBURN ST MARY IS 7 MILES FROM EXETER, JUST NORTH OF THE A30 OKEHAMPTON ROAD, AND IS CLEARLY SIGNPOSTED FROM BOTH DIRECTIONS. THE PUB IS ON THE MAIN STREET, IN THE CENTRE OF THE VILLAGE. **PARKING:** IN THE PUB CAR PARK BUT DO PLEASE ASK FIRST. ALTERNATIVELY, THERE IS ON-STREET PARKING.

Tedburn St Mary is really two villages. What is now the village centre, clustered around the pub, was originally (and logically) known as Taphouse – indeed, it is still referred to as such by the locals. Tedburn St Mary itself is strictly speaking just the area around the parish church, to the north-west. The surrounding area is a patchwork of green fields, hedges and woods cut through by small rivers and streams.

This pleasant and undemanding stroll explores part of this hinterland. A quiet, hedge-fringed lane takes you north to Blackalder Wood, while the return leg follows the valley of the Lilly Brook. It is all easy walking, and the tracks used are easily followed.

The King's Arms Inn

This early 17th century hostelry was originally known as the Taphouse Inn, and was one of a series of alehouses established at approximately 8-mile intervals along the country's main trunk routes for the refreshment of travellers. It was given its present name in a fit of Royalist fervour after the Civil War, when Charles II was believed to have stopped off here on his way west.

It is an attractive and welcoming place, which has retained its thick beams, wooden partitions and leaded windows while making the interior warm and comfortable. The public bar is a plain room with a tiled floor, but the lounge bar is beautifully carpeted and comfortably furnished and has a log fire in winter. There is also a light, airy restaurant, and a beer garden to the rear completes the accommodation.

The menu is very varied. In addition to soups and snacks (try the Stilton mushrooms), a range of steaks, fish and vegetarian dishes is offered, as well as specials such as steak and ale pie. There is an equally impressive array of drinks on tap. Four real ales are always available – Bass is the regular, while the other three change from time to time. The lagers are Carling, Grolsch and Heineken, and you will also find Guinness (both regular and Extra Cold) and Worthington Draught and Creamflow. The King's Arms is open all day from Thursday to Sunday, but closed in the afternoon from Monday to Wednesday. Telephone: 01647 61224.

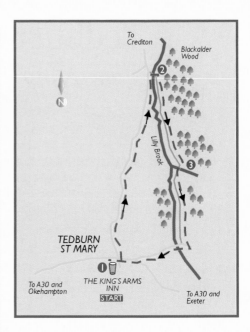

The Walk

① Cross the main road and follow the road immediately opposite the pub (signposted to Crediton). It takes you out of the village and along a lane lined with hedges and a beautiful array of wild flowers in season. As you go, you get a very pleasant view of a patchwork of fields and woods over the hedge on your right. The lane dips and climbs gently in an almost straight line, and after a while you get another good view up ahead.

② About $1\frac{1}{2}$ miles after leaving Tedburn, and after a fairly long and steady descent, you will find a public bridleway sign pointing sharp right, just before a barn and a bridge. Turn here, onto a track. After about 100 yards, cross the Lilly Brook via a footbridge, and at the fork on the other side go right. At the next fork go right again, through a gate. This leads you onto another track along the edge of a wood,

The Lilly Brook

with the brook on the other side of a meadow on your right.

The wood opens up and you will find a field stretching up on your left beyond a belt of trees. Go through another gate and continue along the track on the other side and back into the pretty wood. Another gate follows and soon after that you come to a junction: one track leads to the left up a hill and a second goes sharp right, down to the brook. Take the one in the middle, which goes straight on. After a while you will see the brook sparkling through the trees on the right.

③ About 150 yards after the junction you will find a gate on your right; go through, cross a footbridge and climb to a track by a farm. Bear right here and at the next junction go left. After another 750 yards you join another track; bear right and follow it for a short distance to a road. Turn right to return to Tedburn, and at the junction in the village bear right again to get to the pub.

PLACES OF INTEREST NEARBY

Exeter, with its cathedral, museums and ancient city walls, lies 7 miles to the east of Tedburn St Mary. About the same distance to the south-west is the National Trust property of **Castle Drogo**, perched high above the beautiful Teign Gorge.

Exeter
The Prospect Inn

DIRECTIONS TO START: THE PROSPECT INN IS ON THE QUAY, NEAR EXETER CITY CENTRE.
PARKING: THERE IS NO PUB CAR PARK. FOLLOW THE SIGNS FOR THE CATHEDRAL AND QUAY
CAR PARK. ON LEAVING THE CAR PARK, FOLLOW THE PEDESTRIAN SIGNS FOR THE QUAY AND
THE RIVERSIDE DOWN A SET OF STEPS; THE PUB IS ON THE LEFT AT THE BOTTOM.

Exeter has a history stretching back to Roman times and is home to many architectural gems, including the magnificent Norman cathedral. The Quay is a particularly attractive area which has been very sympathetically restored. Now a peaceful haven, it was once a bustling maritime centre with ships discharging cargoes from Europe and beyond.

This is where the River Exe gives birth to the Exeter Canal, a short waterway built in the 16th century to circumvent a series of weirs which had been erected by the Earls of Devon some centuries earlier to strangle Exeter's trade and force all ships to unload at their own quay further downriver. This easy stroll follows surfaced paths along the left bank of the river before crossing and returning alongside the canal, with a wealth of birdlife to be seen on the water.

The Prospect Inn

Built on two levels and with some delightful little nooks, this lovely 17th century inn has an intimate atmosphere which belies its size. It has the low ceilings and blackened beams one would expect in a building of this age, as well as its own resident ghost – a young girl who was found hanged in mysterious circumstances some centuries ago. It is right on The Quay, and there are tables outside, overlooking the river and the canal basin beyond – a delightful place to relax in warm weather and indulge in a spot of 'people-watching'.

The pub is open all day. The food is all freshly prepared, and ranges from sandwiches and jacket potatoes to pasta, fish, vegetarian and meat dishes, including the mouthwatering pork, apple and cider pie, as well as a variety of daily specials. There is an equally varied array of beers on offer: the local Otter Ale, Wadworth 6X, Bass, London Pride, Whitbread Best, Heineken, Labatt's and Murphy's. Telephone: 01392 273152.

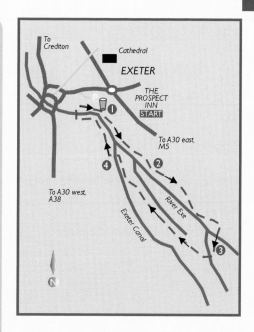

– the two forks soon join up again. Cross a small road.

② At the path junction, go straight on. The path veers slightly away from the river and you cross a small road. After about 400 yards you will find yourself back alongside the river again. You emerge at a road; cross to a small lane straight ahead and follow that. It bends right and ends at a small bridge across a leat.

The Walk

① Turn left as you leave the pub and follow The Quay past a row of 19th-century warehouses, followed by some storage vaults built into the cliff – now used mainly as craft shops. You will meet a road, which soon curves away to the left; continue straight on along the riverbank, through a gate. The path crosses a footbridge over a small inlet by a weir. When it forks you can go either way

③ Cross it and go half left across a field to a path; bear right to cross another bridge, this time over the river. Follow the path round to the right on the other side. At the path junction go straight on (signposted to Exe Bridges and the city centre). You pass some playing fields on the left, with a good view ahead to the cathedral, and then cross another path.

The River Exe

④ About 200 yards further on, go left across a lock and then right, following the sign for the canal basin and ferry. Pass the modern Piazza Terracina and follow the river round to the left until you reach the large, blue Cricklepit Bridge. Turn right to cross it, and then right again on the other side. Cross a small footbridge and go through the open transit shed on the other side to reach the Prospect Inn.

PLACES OF INTEREST NEARBY

There are a number of fascinating places to explore in Exeter, including the **city walls** (built by the Romans) and the **cathedral** with its pretty little close. About 7 miles south of the city is **Powderham Castle**, the home of the Earls of Devon, which is open to the public from Sunday to Friday between April and October.

Branscombe
The Fountain Head

MAPS: OS LANDRANGER 192 OR EXPLORER 115 (FORMERLY 30) (GR 187888)

WALK 15

DISTANCE: 4 MILES

DIRECTIONS TO START: BRANSCOMBE IS ABOUT 2$^1/_2$ MILES SOUTH OF THE A3052 BETWEEN SIDMOUTH AND SEATON, AND IS SIGNPOSTED FROM THAT ROAD. **PARKING:** THE PUB CAR PARK IS VERY SMALL SO THE LANDLADY WOULD PREFER CUSTOMERS NOT TO LEAVE THEIR CARS THERE WHILE WALKING. YOU SHOULD THEREFORE USE THE PUBLIC CAR PARK BY THE VILLAGE HALL (GR 197887) AND IT IS FROM THERE THAT THE ROUTE DESCRIPTION BEGINS.

Branscombe is a long village running down the valley of the same name. In fact, it is really five hamlets – accurately if unimaginatively called Street, Church, Bridge, Vicarage and Great Seaside – separated by farmland.

This delightfully varied walk takes you through Bridge and Church to the Fountain Head in Street, and then across to the Coast Path. It emerges on the cliff above the beach at Great Seaside. There are some stunning coastal and country views along the way.

The Fountain Head

This homely, atmospheric inn gives the impression of having changed little in its 500-year history. It has two bars, one of which was the village smithy until the middle of the last century. Most of the pub has stone floors and dark panelled walls, although the back bar is carpeted. There are more tables outside in the courtyard.

The pub's four real ales are all produced by the local Branscombe Vale Brewery, and delicious they are too. Carlsberg and Stella Artois are the draught lagers. Good traditional pub food is served here, ranging from snacks and sandwiches to chicken, fish and vegetarian main courses and daily specials. Monday to Saturday opening hours are 11.30 am to 2.30 pm and 6.30 pm to 11 pm, with the normal, more restricted hours on Sundays. Telephone: 01297 680359.

The Walk

① Turn right as you leave the car park, and follow the lane through the village, passing the Old Bakery tearoom on your left and the Forge on your right. You will then come to the church on your left, followed by the magnificent Millennium Rose Garden, also on your left, and a lovely row of cottages on your right. About 3/4 mile after leaving the car park, you will pass a small lane on your left; just beyond it is the Fountain Head.

② On leaving the Fountain Head turn right through the pub car park, and when you reach the lane beyond turn left, and almost immediately right through a gate

onto a path. There is a public footpath sign, but it is hidden by a hedge. Cross a stile and follow the path into a wood. At the end of the wood cross another stile into a field; keep to the left alongside a hedge.

Go through a gap in the hedge ahead of you and continue along the path (signposted to the cliff). Follow a rough track round to the right until you meet another track; turn left (signposted to the Coast Path). Go through a gate and follow the track straight on (signposted to Branscombe Mouth). You are now on the Coast Path.

③ Follow the track into a lovely wood. You come out into a field, and then cross a stile into the wood again. About 1/2 mile after joining the Coast Path, you emerge onto the cliff top, to be met by a superb view along the beach ahead. Go down some steps, followed by a steep path and then some more steps to a kissing-gate. Cross the next field and go through a gateway on your right. Bear right across the next field to another kissing-gate and then go down to the left past a shop and café to a car park.

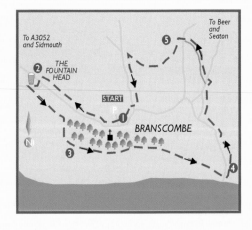

Great Seaside

④ Just beyond the car park is a lane; follow it up the hill to the left. After about 600 yards you will come to a small lane going off to the right; follow that for 250 yards until it emerges onto a road. Turn right and then left into another lane.

After 100 yards or so you pass a small track going off to the left; carry straight on along the surfaced lane. After a while it becomes an unsurfaced track and enters another pretty wood. You eventually cross a small ford; turn left into the lane beyond. Pass the drive for Gay's Farm and a few yards further on you will come to another drive on the right.

⑤ Turn up here – there is a public footpath sign, but it is hidden in the hedge. Pass a house on your right and an old farm building on your left, and cross a cattle-grid into a green lane. After a little more than 100 yards, as the green lane swings left, you will see a yellow waymark pointing right through a gate; follow it onto a path between high hedges. Go through another gate and turn left.

You emerge into an open field; go straight across it, following the line of electricity poles to a bank and a stile. Turn right on the other side and follow the edge of the field. In the far corner you will find a stile; cross it and turn right along the side of another field. At the end of the hedge turn left across the field to another stile; bear right down the next field to a gate into a lane. Turn left and follow the lane down for about $1/4$ mile to the village hall and the car park.

PLACES OF INTEREST NEARBY

In Branscombe you will find **Manor Mill**, owned by the National Trust, which is open on Wednesday and Sunday afternoons in summer, but only on Sunday afternoons in winter. Not far to the east you will find **Beer Quarry Caves**, a network of caves which were first quarried in Roman times, and which are open to the public in summer.

East Budleigh
The Sir Walter Raleigh

MAPS: OS LANDRANGER 192 OR EXPLORER 115 (FORMERLY 30) (GR 066847)

WALK 16

DISTANCE: 2¾ MILES

DIRECTIONS TO START: EAST BUDLEIGH IS JUST WEST OF THE B3178 BETWEEN NEWTON POPPLEFORD AND BUDLEIGH SALTERTON. FOLLOW THE ROAD INTO THE VILLAGE CENTRE TO REACH THE SIR WALTER RALEIGH. **PARKING:** THE PUB HAS NO CAR PARK OF ITS OWN, BUT THERE IS A FREE PUBLIC CAR PARK 50 YARDS AWAY, DOWN HAYES LANE.

East Budleigh is a very attractive village of thatched and slate-roofed cottages and larger houses. Its most famous son was Sir Walter Raleigh, who was born at Hayes Barton, a mile west of the village, and began his education here. The church, where Raleigh's father was a church-warden, is worth a visit – the pew ends are beautifully carved, and the Raleigh coat of arms can be seen on one of them.

This easy amble follows a quiet lane out to Hayes Barton, a pretty cob and thatch farmhouse, and then takes a farm track up to Hayes Wood, a delightful mixed woodland of conifers and beeches. You join a green lane for a short distance on the return leg, before cutting across more farmland. You get some grand views along the way, and the hedgerows are filled with flowers in spring and summer.

The Sir Walter Raleigh

The village local is a lovely 16th-century inn in the main street, and was probably known to the man after whom it has subsequently been named. It comprises a small bar furnished with padded benches and chairs, and a light and airy non-smoking restaurant. It has the old beams and small windows one associates with the period, and a beer garden has just been added at the back.

The pub prides itself on its hand-pumped beers. Marston's Pedigree is always offered, alongside two guest beers (Charles Wells Bombardier is a particular favourite with the locals, and features quite regularly by popular request). Other beers available on tap are Whitbread Best, Carlsberg and Grolsch lagers and Guinness. The food is excellent and ranges from soup and pâté to main courses such as Chicken Kiev. Fish is a particular speciality. Opening hours are 11.45 am to 3 pm and 6.30 pm to 11 pm (12 noon to 2.30 pm and 7 pm to 10.30 pm on Sundays). Telephone: 01395 442510.

The Walk

① The walk starts immediately opposite the pub, in Hayes Lane. Follow the lane past the car park and cross a stream. As you leave the village, you will pass a house called Vicar's Mead on your left; this is where Raleigh went to school. The lane takes you westwards between high banks, with the occasional view over farmland. It is beautifully quiet out here – only the occasional bird breaks the silence. After $\frac{1}{2}$ mile you come to a junction; carry

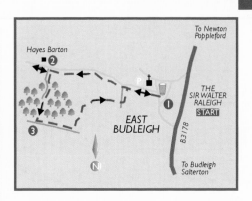

straight on. About $\frac{1}{2}$ mile further on, you will come to the pretty thatched farmhouse of Hayes Barton, Raleigh's birthplace. Please remember that this is a private house, and although you can view it from the road, the house and grounds are not open to the public.

② Retrace your steps for 100 yards to a track going right and a path going left (both indicated by public footpath signs). Turn right up the track, passing some fields of pigs as you go. You pass a house and the track goes to the right. Where it forks, go left, following the yellow waymark, to enter Hayes Wood. Although it is a conifer plantation, the trees are not as tightly packed as in most plantations, and there is more light and undergrowth than usual. At the next fork, take the right-hand route, again following the yellow waymark. This sunken track takes you into an attractive stand of beech trees. Cross another track, still following the yellow waymarks.

③ You eventually emerge into the open and join a green lane; turn left. Follow the pretty track for about $\frac{1}{4}$ mile until you come to public footpaths leading off to left and right. Take the left one, crossing a

Vicar's Mead, where Sir Walter Raleigh was educated

stile and keeping to the left of the field beyond. You get a lovely view over the rolling farms ahead and across to the sea half right. Cross another stile and keep to the left of the next field to a third stile. Follow the right-hand hedge on the other side until you come to one last stile, which takes you onto another green lane. Turn left. The track emerges onto Hayes Lane about 200 yards outside East Budleigh; turn right to return to the village and the pub.

PLACES OF INTEREST NEARBY

Half a mile north of the village is **Bicton Park**, with its acres of beautiful gardens. A mile and a half south you will find the attractive seaside town of **Budleigh Salterton**.

Horndon
The Elephant's Nest

MAPS: OS LANDRANGER 191 OR OUTDOOR LEISURE 28 (GR 517800)	WALK 17	DISTANCE: $3\frac{1}{2}$ MILES

DIRECTIONS TO START: TURN EAST OFF THE A386 TAVISTOCK-OKEHAMPTON ROAD AT MARY TAVY AND FOLLOW THE SIGNS FOR HORNDON. THE PUB IS ON THE RIGHT JUST BEFORE THE HAMLET OF HORNDON ITSELF. **PARKING:** IN THE PUB CAR PARK, BUT PLEASE ASK FIRST. ALTERNATIVELY, PARK NEAR THE COTTAGES AT POINT 3 AND START THE WALK FROM THERE.

Although tin mining was one of the mainstays of the economy of Dartmoor proper, around the edges of the moor it was minerals like copper, lead, silver and arsenic that predominated. This corner of the national park was home to three major mines: Wheal Jewell, where the original tin extraction was followed by arsenic; Wheal Betsy, which produced copper, lead, silver and arsenic; and Wheal Friendship, where copper and lead were followed by arsenic.

Views are a major attraction of the route: there are some superb panoramas over Dartmoor, both to the south and to the east. It also follows a delightful, tree-shrouded leat above the River Tavy along the way. It is all easy walking, but note that at the end of the leat you have to climb a ladder to reach the lane above.

The Elephant's Nest

This 16th century building was once a row of miners' cottages; it has only been a pub since the 19th century. It is a lovely stone building, with an open fireplace at one end of the main bar and two interconnecting rooms at the other. There is also a large beer garden.

Originally called the New Inn, the pub derives its unusual name from a previous landlord, who was noted for his enormous size. As he sat on his stool behind the bar one evening, one of his regulars commented that he looked like an elephant on a nest. It is open from 11.30 am to 2.30 pm and 6.30 pm to 11 pm on Monday to Saturday, and at the usual restricted hours on Sunday.

The Elephant's Nest has won awards for its ales and its food. There are always two guest beers to try, in addition to the regular West Country ales: Hicks Special Draught from St Austell and Palmers IPA. Also available are Boddingtons Draught, Stella Artois and Heineken lager, Harvest Dry and Stowford Press cider and Guinness. The extensive food menu changes regularly, but might include exotic offerings such as wild boar and roast quail as well as simpler meals like filled baguettes and delicious home-made soup. Telephone: 01822 810273.

The Walk

① Turn right and follow the lane for 200 yards to a junction; turn right. At the next junction, go right again. When the lane ends, carry straight on along a green lane. After 150 yards you will find a stile on your

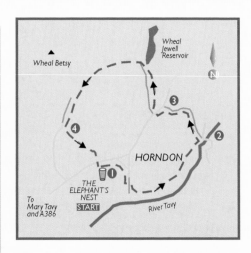

left by a leat; cross it and follow the path alongside the leat. You pass some small stone clapper bridges across the leat and cross a few more stiles before emerging alongside the river at the weir below Hill Bridge.

② Alongside the bridge is a metal ladder up to the lane above; climb it and turn left along the lane. After a few yards go through the gate to Hill Bridge Farm, following the public bridlepath sign for Creason. Follow the drive on the other side through another gate. Pass the farm and go through another gate. Bear left on the other side (*not* through the gate marked Lower Town). The track swings to the left and then to the right and goes through another gate, emerging onto an open down. Follow it along the edge of the down, and round to the right at the end.

③ The track comes out at a road; turn left (signposted to Horndon and Mary Tavy). After 200 yards you will see another track going sharp right opposite some cottages; turn along it. Dotted around on the right of the track are some of the old mine

Hill Bridge, on the River Tavy

shafts that formed the Wheal Jewell complex. After 600 yards or so you will come to the rather ugly-looking pumping station of Wheal Jewell Reservoir.

Turn left opposite the pumping station and make your way across the open moor. There is no clear path, but it is easy to see where you are going; simply aim for the corner of the wall about 250 yards ahead. Follow the wall round to the left; as you go, you will see the remains of the engine house of Wheal Betsy half right. In the far corner you will come to a gate; go through and follow the track on the other side down to a surfaced lane.

④ Pass Kingsett farmhouse, and when the lane turns right you will see a public footpath sign pointing through the farmyard on the left to the Elephant's Nest. Turn into the farmyard and at the end go right and then left between the barns and sheds and through a gate. Bear right across the field beyond to a stile in the corner. Cross it and the small footbridge on the other side. Bear left and make your way to the end of the wall ahead of you. Cross it via stone steps set into it and keep to the left of the field beyond. At the end, cross the next wall and a fence and keep to the left of the next field. Cross the next wall and fence. Bear left across the next field, cross another wall, keep to the left of another field and cross the final wall into the lane opposite the pub.

PLACES OF INTEREST NEARBY

Five miles north of Horndon, just off the A386, is **Lydford Gorge**, a superb wooded valley owned by the National Trust. A similar distance to the south is the market town of **Tavistock**.

Near Postbridge
The Warren House Inn

MAPS: OS LANDRANGER 191 OR OUTDOOR LEISURE 28 (GR 674809)

WALK 18

DISTANCE: 4 MILES

DIRECTIONS TO START: THE PUB IS 2 MILES NORTH-EAST OF POSTBRIDGE ON THE B3212 PRINCETOWN-MORETONHAMPSTEAD ROAD. **PARKING:** IN THE KING'S OVEN CAR PARK, 200 YARDS UP THE ROAD TOWARDS MORETONHAMPSTEAD.

Dartmoor was at one time a major tin-mining area – indeed, the ore was mined on the moor for some 800 years, right up to the beginning of the 20th century. The earliest miners extracted the ore from streams, leaving piles of waste along the banks as their only memorials. As the streams became less productive, they began to dig into the hillsides in search of the precious metal, creating deep gullies, known locally as girts. The industry's final phase came with the Industrial Revolution, when large-scale extraction from deep shafts became possible.

This walk enables you to explore the tin workings of this area, and gives you a taste of the grandeur of Dartmoor without too much effort. It takes you down into the valley of the infant West Webburn River and then circles round the hill opposite, via farm tracks and paths, returning across the open moor. There are some lovely views along the way, and in summer the slopes are a purple mass of heather.

The Warren House Inn

The maxim 'Don't judge a book by its cover' was never more true than in the case of the Warren House. Its austere, exposed, weather-beaten façade hides a cheerful, comfortable interior where you can be sure of a warm welcome and good sustenance. The present inn was built in 1845 to replace an older one on the other side of the road, which served the tin miners in the valley below.

There is just the one bar, with a granite fireplace at each end. There is a children's room at one end of the bar, and tables and benches out on the moor across the road. The pub is open all day in summer, but closes in the afternoon from November to February.

There are usually four real ales available at any one time; among them when I last visited were Butcombe Bitter and Tanglefoot. Other draught offerings include Stella Artois and Carlsberg lagers, Murphy's stout and Strongbow cider. The food is delicious, and ranges from sandwiches and jacket potatoes to home-made pies, including the rabbit-based Warrener's Pie. Telephone: 01822 880208.

The Walk

① Starting from the pub, cross the road onto the open moor and head downhill, bearing slightly left. Just to the left of a group of trees you will see a gap in the wall ahead of you; go through that and follow the path on the other side through the bracken. When you come to a fork, keep straight on, along the broader path. Soon the bracken gives way to heather and you

---

PLACES OF INTEREST NEARBY

Just above Headland Warren Farm are the remains of the Bronze Age settlement of **Grimspound**, and about 4 miles away, near Moretonhampstead, is the **Miniature Pony Centre**.

---

come to a broad track; bear right and follow it down into the valley. Where the track bends to the left, take the path that goes straight on.

② Cross over the little stream at the bottom and turn right onto the track beyond. After 500 yards you go through a gate and continue along a somewhat rougher track on the other side. This section can be a bit wet at first, but it is quite passable and soon becomes drier.

③ At the junction, go straight on (signposted to the road near Headland Warren via Challacombe). After a few yards you cross another track; go straight on again. You pass the remains of the Golden Dagger Mine, and at the next junction bear left, following the public footpath sign, and cross a stile. (There is a sign on the gate alongside indicating that this is the footpath to Challacombe.) A broad grassy path takes you up a slight incline and you will eventually find a fence on your right. Further on you will find a gorse hedge on your left, and the path runs between the fence and the hedge to a gate.

④ On the other side you join a track; bear left (signposted to the road near Headland Warren). Go through another gate and past some farm buildings and a house onto a drive. Where the drive

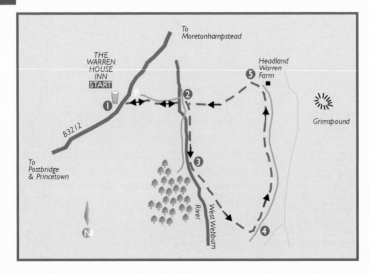

on your right and go through another gate.

⑤ At the fingerpost on the other side turn left (signposted to the Warren House Inn again). Follow the well-worn path to the right of some girts and after a little more than $1/2$ mile you will come to a track. You are now on the path you came out on. Bear right along the track, and then after a few yards turn left to cross the stream and follow the path up the hillside on the other side. When the path joins the track, bear left, and at the top of the climb you will see the broad path you followed from the pub leading half left. Turn off here to return to the Warren House Inn, or continue along the track to reach the car park.

swings right, go straight on through a gate. You pass some cottages and go through another gate. The track across the field beyond is not very clear at first, but it is possible to make out its line and it soon becomes much more distinct. Follow it for $1/2$ mile or so to a gate; go through and continue for another 500 yards to Headland Warren Farm. Go through another gate and straight on (signposted to the Warren House Inn). Pass the farm

Tin-mining remains, Dartmoor

Kenton
The Devon Arms

MAPS: OS LANDRANGER 192 OR EXPLORER 110 (FORMERLY 31) (GR 959832)

WALK 19

DISTANCE: 3½ MILES

DIRECTIONS TO START: THE A379 EXETER-DAWLISH ROAD PASSES THROUGH KENTON, AND THE DEVON ARMS IS IN THE CENTRE OF THE VILLAGE. **PARKING:** IN THE PUB CAR PARK, BUT PLEASE ASK FIRST. ALTERNATIVELY, THERE IS A FREE PUBLIC CAR PARK A FEW YARDS UP THE ROAD.

The Exe is world renowned for its birdlife; in winter, up to 20,000 birds of 30 species can be seen on the sand and mud of the estuary at any one time, and about 180 species are recorded in the area each year. And Kenton is an ideal base for exploring the upper reaches of the estuary. Not far from the river, it is a quiet backwater, with a pleasant blend of traditional, Victorian and modern housing.

This attractive route is full of interest. A quiet lane, flower-fringed for much of the year, takes you to the waterside village of Starcross, from where you follow the river upstream to the Powderham estate, with a chance to see its famous herd of deer (and a multitude of pheasants). A pretty path crosses the estate to return you to Kenton. It is all easy walking, most of it along lanes, and in addition to the river, the birds and the deer there are some excellent views to enjoy along the way.

The Devon Arms

This delightful old coaching house dates back to the 16th century, although it did not become an inn until much later. There are two bars, both with plushly upholstered furniture and blackened beams, and both decorated with old farm implements and prints. The lounge bar has a dining area attached, and a lovely stone fireplace. The public bar is set up for games, with both darts and pool. There is also a pretty garden at the side, with a children's play area and a small aviary.

The pub is open at the usual times (closed in the afternoons), and offers a range of beers on tap. The cask ales are Marston's Pedigree, Wadworth 6X and Teign Valley Tipple, a local brew. Also available are Whitbread Best bitter, Stella Artois, Heineken and Foster's lagers and Guinness. The food is equally wide-ranging. In addition to sandwiches, jacket potatoes and other snacks, you will find a variety of steak, fish and vegetarian dishes, as well as a daily curry, a daily soup and other specials. Telephone: 01626 890213.

The Walk

① Turn left along the main A379, and after 50 yards, just beyond the Forge, turn right along a surfaced path which soon brings you out at a small road. At the T-junction at the end, turn left and climb out of the village. When the lane swings right, follow it round, and at the junction about 300 yards further on, go straight on (signposted to Starcross). You come over a rise and are met by a good view of the Exe estuary – which gets even better as you go

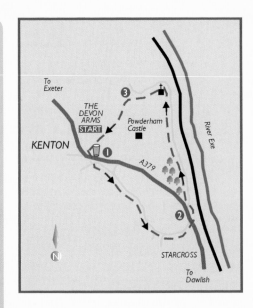

along. At the next junction go straight on again, and at the T-junction 300 yards beyond it, bear left. The new lane takes you into the outskirts of Starcross; ignore the turnings to left and right and keep to the main lane as it twists among the houses.

② You come out onto the A379; cross to a car park. Turn left and cross a grassed picnic area to a gate. Bear right along a lane, with a wood on your left and a railway line and the river on your right. After a little while the wood gives way to parkland and you will see Powderham Castle in the distance half left. You should soon be able to see the estate's herd of deer browsing in the park alongside the lane. A little over a mile from Starcross, the lane turns sharp left past Powderham church. Follow it round.

③ When the lane turns sharp right again, go straight on across a large grass verge to a kissing-gate. Climb along the left-hand

The belvedere at Powderham

edge of the field; as you do so, you will get a good view on your left, over the Powderham estate to the Exe estuary. Go through a kissing-gate at the end of the field, and follow the path on the other side between a fence and a wood, down to a drive. You may well find pheasants darting about all around you along this stretch.

Cross the drive and go down to a gate and across a narrow-gauge steam railway line. Go over a footbridge across the River Kenn. It is hard to imagine that this trickle of water was once a navigable river, and Kenton a thriving trading centre, with boats plying to and fro to the coast. At the path junction on the other side go straight on. Cross a narrow lane and go through a gate. Another gate at the end of the path takes you to the main road; turn left to return to the Devon Arms.

PLACES OF INTEREST NEARBY

Powderham Castle, the home of the Earl of Devon, whose estate you have just crossed, is open to the public; the entrance is on the A379 just south-east of Kenton. Four miles south of the village is the nature reserve of **Dawlish Warren**, while **Exeter**, 6 miles in the other direction, offers attractions of a different kind: a cathedral, museums and centuries of history.

Whitchurch
The Whitchurch Inn

MAPS: OS LANDRANGER 201 OR OUTDOOR LEISURE 28 (GR 492726)

WALK 20

DISTANCE: $3^1/_2$ MILES

DIRECTIONS TO START: WHITCHURCH IS A SMALL VILLAGE ON THE SOUTH-EASTERN OUTSKIRTS OF TAVISTOCK. IT IS SIGNPOSTED FROM TAVISTOCK AND FROM THE A386 JUST SOUTH OF THE TOWN. ONCE YOU GET TO THE VILLAGE, YOU WILL FIND THE PUB CLEARLY SIGNPOSTED.
PARKING: THERE IS NO PUB CAR PARK, SO PARK WITH CARE ALONG THE ROAD.

Although Whitchurch is just outside the Dartmoor National Park, most of this walk is within the park's boundaries. There is a bit of climbing as you go, but nothing too strenuous. Whitchurch itself is worth exploring; there are some lovely cottages and houses, and the beautiful 13th century church deserves a visit.

The main attraction of this route, however, is the opportunity it provides to experience the seemingly unbounded expanse of the moor and feel its tranquillity and silence. You only skirt its fringe, but the open spaces of Plaster Down, in the middle of the walk, and the views across the hills and tors from there, will give you a taste of the pleasures on offer further out.

The Whitchurch Inn

Built by monks in the 13th century, this delightful little inn originally served as a church house, providing hospitality to travellers and those visiting the church next door. It also acted as the church's administrative offices, and the restaurant at the back used to be the tithe room, where parishioners came to pay their tithes. It is now a snug, cosy pub with beautiful old oak beams, leaded windows and an open fireplace. The tradition of welcoming visitors continues; it is a warm, friendly place, with a quiet, understated charm.

Open all day, the inn offers a wide range of food, from snacks and sandwiches to main courses such as lasagne and salmon steaks. There are three regular real ales – Hicks, Fuller's London Pride and Bass – and one guest beer. Also on tap are Worthington Cream Flow, Caffrey's, Carling and Stella Artois lagers, Blackthorn cider and Guinness. Telephone: 01822 612181.

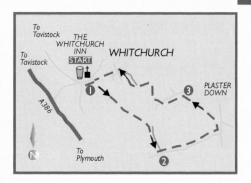

The Walk

NB: A short stretch of the route (in point 3) is a bit rough and rocky underfoot, so stout shoes or boots are recommended.

① As you leave the pub, turn left and pass the church. Immediately opposite the end of the church, you will find a kissing-gate, with two public footpath signs. Go through and turn right. Make your way across a field and down a fairly steep hill. In the far corner you will find a footbridge and a stile. Cross both and keep to the left-hand side of the field beyond.

Climb to a gap in the bank ahead and cross the next field to a stone stile. Bear left across another field to the corner of the hedge; go through a gate and follow the left-hand hedge of yet another field to another stile. Keep to the left again on the other side to yet another stile. Go diagonally left across the next field and go through a gateway. Keep slightly to the right of the left-hand boundary of the field beyond to reach a gate and stile. On the other side, bear right to a metal barrier and cross the next field to a gap in the corner of a bank. Bear right, go through a gate and across a footbridge. You come to a second gate with a stile alongside. Keep to the left of the field on the other side and cross one more stile to reach a farm drive. Turn right and follow the drive for about $^1/_4$ mile to a cattle-grid and a gate leading onto a lane.

② Turn left and follow the lane for a little over $^1/_2$ mile. It is beautifully peaceful out here; the only sounds are the rustling of the wind and the occasional birdsong. There is also a rich variety of hedgerow flowers to enjoy as you pass. You finally come out onto Plaster Down, the beginning of Dartmoor proper, and join a

Looking towards Pew Tor

road; turn left. You now get a magnificent view across the moor, with a number of tors visible on the horizon. Follow the road for 100 yards to a junction; immediately opposite the junction, bear left away from the road, following the wall.

③ At the end of the wall, after ½ mile or so, you come to a lane; turn left. Ignore the turning off to the right; continue along the lane for about 200 yards until it emerges onto another patch of heathland. You get more good views here, over to the

moors on your right and across into Cornwall ahead of you. Leave the road and follow the wall on your right. When it goes to the right follow it round, and at the bottom, where it goes left, follow it round again.

In the far corner you will find a gate on your right, leading into a green lane. Go through and follow the lane. It is rather rocky, so take care as you make your way down. After about 300 yards it emerges through a gate onto a lane; turn left. At the crossroads, go straight on past some houses. When the lane curves to the left and ends, go straight on along a clear path, through a gate and into a field. Continue along the path across the field to the kissing-gate opposite the church; turn left to return to the pub.

> ### PLACES OF INTEREST NEARBY
> About 4 miles to the south along the A386, just outside **Yelverton**, you will find a **museum of paperweights**.

Bovey Tracey
The Old Thatched Inn

<table>
<tr><td>MAPS: OS LANDRANGER 191 OR EXPLORER 110 (FORMERLY 31) (GR 813781)</td><td>WALK 21</td><td>DISTANCE: 3¼ MILES</td></tr>
</table>

DIRECTIONS TO START: TURN OFF THE A38 AT THE DRUM BRIDGES EXIT AND FOLLOW THE SIGNS FOR BOVEY TRACEY ALONG THE A382. TURN RIGHT AT THE SECOND ROUNDABOUT TOWARDS THE TOWN CENTRE AND THE PUB IS ON THE RIGHT. **PARKING:** THERE IS A PUBLIC CAR PARK ALONGSIDE THE PUB.

Bovey Tracey is a pleasant little town straddling the River Bovey, which gives it its name. It is particularly well placed for exploring south-eastern Dartmoor. Just outside the town is Parke, a National Trust estate which houses the headquarters of the National Park Authority, and just down the road from the Old Thatched Inn is the Riverside Centre, a converted mill which houses the Devon Guild of Craftsmen.

A more idyllic place than Parke would be hard to find: a delightful mixed wood stretching up a hill with a small river tumbling and murmuring softly below. This lovely amble takes you through a pretty park to the estate, where you follow a woodland path above the river, returning along the riverbank. With excellent views, a magnificent variety of wild flowers in season and a disused railway line to enjoy along the way, this route has it all.

The Old Thatched Inn

This pretty 17th-century coaching inn has been very well preserved and decorated, and retains its traditional charm. It comprises three rooms. There is the delightful old bar, with a non-smoking dining room alongside and a large chimney in between, with stone fireplaces on both sides. The floor is also of stone and there are low oak beams. Off the bar is a games room, and a pleasant beer garden at the rear completes the accommodation.

The food is all good pub grub, and ranges from ploughman's lunches and sandwiches to scampi and chips or bangers and mash. They are particularly proud of their cask ales: Greene King Abbot Ale is the regular offering, and there are always two others, of different strengths, available. Also on tap are Tetley's Smoothflow, Ansell's, Stella Artois and Carlsberg lagers and Blackthorn cider. The inn is open during the standard hours in the week, but all day at weekends. Telephone: 01626 833421.

The Walk

① Cross the road and turn right. Just before the bridge across the River Bovey, turn left into a park. (On the other side of the river, on the right, is the Devon Guild of Craftsmen's Riverside Centre.) You pass a children's play area, and later some playing fields, all the time with the river on your right.

② After about ¼ mile, you go through a gate and come to the main road. Cross with care and go through a kissing-gate on the other side. Bear right along a track, which is the route of a disused railway line. After about 150 yards you cross the river and come to some steps on the left; go down and across a stile. You now have the river on your left. Cross another stile and enter a wood, following the river. Go down some steps on your left and cross a small footbridge to a field. Bear left to a stone bridge.

③ Follow a track on the other side, which climbs a hill between fields. Just before you come to a gate, turn right up some steps and through a gate, following the sign for the woodland walk. Follow the clear path as it curves up to the left. It leads you through a beautiful mixed wood

The Riverside Centre, home of the Devon Guild of Craftsmen

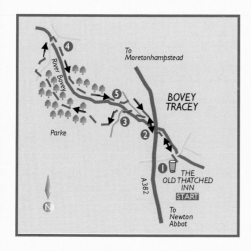

at any time of year, but with the sunlight filtering through the trees and dappling the water in summer and a beautiful array of flowers alongside the path it is magical. The Himalayan balsam, although it can be an invasive pest, is particularly attractive on this stretch when it is in flower. You eventually cross a boardwalk on your left and then bear right, leaving the river and crossing a field.

⑤ When you come to a track, turn left, following the sign to the railway walk, and follow it up to a stile. On the other side you rejoin the disused railway; turn right. At the end, go through the kissing-gate you came through on the way out. Cross the main road, go through the gate on the other side and cross the park to return to the pub.

high above the river, and from time to time the trees open up on the right to give you a superb view across the valley. After a little over $^1/_2$ mile the path ends at a gate; go through into a lane and turn right. Cross the river and at the junction go straight on.

④ Just before the T-junction, turn right through a kissing-gate and follow the path up to the disused railway. At the top, cross the track and follow a path down to the river; turn left and follow the riverbank. After a while you go through two kissing-gates. It is lovely along here

PLACES OF INTEREST NEARBY
The **Devon Guild of Craftsmen's Riverside Centre** has displays and sales of work by a wide range of craftsmen, from needleworkers to potters and woodturners. Also in Bovey Tracey are the **Cardew Tea Pottery**, where you can see novelty teapots being made, and the **House of Marbles** glassworks.

Meavy
The Royal Oak

MAPS: OS LANDRANGER 201 (START AND FINISH), 202 (MIDDLE) OR OUTDOOR LEISURE 28 (GR 541672)

WALK 22

DISTANCE: 3¼ MILES

DIRECTIONS TO START: TURN EAST OFF THE A386 AT THE ROUNDABOUT AT YELVERTON AND FOLLOW THE SIGNS. ALTERNATIVELY, IF YOU ARE APPROACHING FROM DARTMOOR, TURN LEFT OFF THE B3212 AT DOUSLAND. **PARKING:** ROUND THE VILLAGE GREEN OUTSIDE THE PUB, OR BEHIND THE PARISH HALL ON THE OPPOSITE SIDE OF THE GREEN.

Burrator Reservoir, a large man-made lake surrounded by woods, is a beautiful spot, very popular with visitors. Meavy, just downstream from the dam outlet, on the river of the same name, is an attractive little village with a traditional green at its heart. Alongside the green is the 500-year-old oak tree which gives the pub its name (although why it should be 'royal' is uncertain).

This is a delightful and varied walk which links the village with the reservoir. The route takes you up to the open heathland of Yennadon Down, with magnificent views through 360 degrees. It then enters the open conifer woods around the reservoir and follows the route of a disused railway before emerging at the dam wall. The return leg is through more woodland, this time broadleaved.

The Royal Oak

This friendly old inn opens onto the village green, which is ideal in good weather as it means customers can enjoy their drinks outside in the sun. Even if the weather is not conducive to sitting outside, however, the interior of the inn is full of character and atmosphere, with low beams and leaded windows.

The food is excellent – and makes use of local, organic produce wherever possible. The steaks and gammon are all locally reared, and the fish comes straight from the dock at Plymouth daily. For those who want something a little less substantial, there is a range of bar snacks, from jacket potatoes and salads to pasties and filled baguettes. The resident cask ales are Bass and two local brews: Dartmoor IPA and Jail Ale from Princetown. There is also a guest beer, and other draught offerings are Guinness, Carling lager, Worthington Best bitter, Mitchells and Butlers mild, Westons scrumpy and Blackthorn cider. Opening times are 11.30 am to 3 pm and 6.30 pm to 11 pm, with the usual shorter Sunday hours. Telephone: 01822 852944.

The Walk

① Take the lane that goes left from the pub, and follow it round to the left to leave the village. It climbs between high banks for about 500 yards. At the T-junction at the top, cross the road and go through a gate onto Yennadon Down. Take the left-hand track, the less distinct of the two, on the other side and climb gently for 100 yards or so to a stone footbridge across

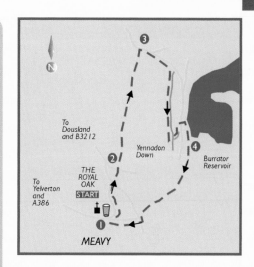

a dry leat. Continue for a few more yards to a road.

② On the other side, find your own way across the open down; there is no particular path to follow, but as long as you keep going roughly straight on and do not cross any walls or fences, you cannot go wrong. If you are concerned about getting lost, then simply keep to the boundary on the left. You cross a track, which is the route of the dismantled Plymouth and Dartmoor Railway, and keep climbing gently through the gorse.

③ After a mile (a little more if you have been following the boundary), you will come to a road; turn right. At the fork, go right, following the main road, to enter an attractive conifer wood. About 200 yards further on, you will find a path leading off

PLACES OF INTEREST NEARBY
Two miles beyond Yelverton, on the other side of the A386, is **Buckland Abbey**, a National Trust property which was once home to Sir Francis Drake.

The dam wall, Burrator Reservoir

to the right, marked with a post with a purple circle on it. Turn off here and bear left to join the track of the disused railway just after it crosses the road. (If you reach the point where the road goes under the disused railway, you have gone too far, and will have to clamber up the bank on the right to reach it.)

Bear right along the track, and after 200 yards you go through a gate. After 500 yards you pass a stone building and go through another gate. About 200 yards beyond the gate you will see some steps on your right and some more, less obvious, on your left; go down the left-hand ones to a track. Turn left again and follow the track to a road.

④ Turn sharp right and follow the road alongside the reservoir. At the junction by the dam wall, go straight on. You pass some toilets on your left; immediately beyond them, turn left onto a track (signposted to Meavy). When the track turns sharp left, go straight on along a path alongside a dry leat. Where the path is blocked by a bank bear left, leaving the leat and following the yellow waymarks painted on some of the trees. You follow the bank for a short distance and then bear left downhill through the wood, still looking out for the yellow waymarks on the trees.

Where the path forks, go left; the junction is not very clear, but there are still waymarks on the trees. Even if you do miss it it does not matter, as you will soon come to a fence, which you can follow down to the left to rejoin the route. The path comes out at a track; bear right to a gate, followed after a few yards by another one. Continue along the track through another stretch of woodland until you emerge through a gap in a bank into a field. Where the track turns left, go straight on to another gate into a lane. Turn left and immediately right, and follow this lane into the centre of Meavy and the pub across the green on the right.

Newton Abbot
The Jolly Farmer

MAPS: OS LANDRANGER 202 OR EXPLORER 110 (FORMERLY 31) (GR 858712)

WALK 23

DISTANCE: 2^1/$_2$ MILES

DIRECTIONS TO START: NEWTON ABBOT LIES JUST OFF THE A380 EXETER-TORQUAY ROAD AND NOT FAR FROM THE A38 DEVON EXPRESSWAY. THE JOLLY FARMER IS IN MARKET STREET, CLOSE TO THE MARKET ITSELF. **PARKING:** IN THE MULTISTOREY PUBLIC CAR PARK ABOUT 50 YARDS FROM THE PUB.

Newton Abbot is a pleasant market town which is divided in two by the River Lemon – indeed, it was originally two towns – Newton Bushel to the north of the river and Newton Abbot to the south. Although the market area has been redeveloped, the market itself is full of interest and draws visitors from far and wide. The town also manages to support an amazing number of pubs; there are seventeen in the town centre alone – an area no more than ^{1}/$_4$ mile square!

This easy stroll takes you from one of these hostelries along the Lemon to the National Trust property of Bradley Manor and the delightful Bradley Wood. The return leg takes in one of the most beautiful churchyards to be seen in Devon, and includes some superb views across to Dartmoor.

The Jolly Farmer

This is an attractive, L-shaped pub, quite large but with snug little alcoves and nooks which give it a surprisingly intimate atmosphere. Over 200 years old and originally a hotel, it has been extensively but sympathetically converted to give it the ambience of a traditional pub, with exposed brickwork (including the bar counter) and dark beams which are matched by the outside shutters. There is a pretty courtyard and arbour at the back.

An impressive variety of drinks is on tap, including beers such as Wychwood Hobgoblin and Bass, John Smith's Extra Smooth, Courage Best, Foster's, Kronenbourg and Stella Artois lager, Scrumpy Jack and Strongbow cider and Guinness. The food is equally varied. It is all home-made and ranges from baguettes and 'doorsteps' (thick crusty sandwiches) to international delights such as balti and Mexican dishes, as well as traditional British fare. The Jolly Farmer is open all day, every day. Telephone: 01626 354010.

The Walk

① From the pub, cross Market Street and turn left to pass the library. Follow the road round to the right, and at the pedestrian lights cross the road and turn left and then right into a small lane alongside the river. When the lane bears right into a car park, go straight on along a path by the riverside. As you go, you pass some industrial units on your right.

② After about 500 yards, your path joins another; turn right and after a few yards left along a track. You pass another track

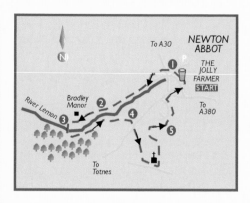

going off to the right; carry straight on and you will come to a gate leading into the grounds of Bradley Manor. Carry straight on, with the river on your left, and the leat that used to serve Bradley Mill on your right. Cross the drive to Bradley Manor (the manor itself is largely hidden by hedges and trees), and follow a surfaced path alongside the leat.

③ When the meadow narrows, you will see a footbridge across the river on your left; cross it into Bradley Wood and turn left. A number of paths lead off to the right; ignore them and keep to the riverside until you come to a kissing-gate. Go through it and keep to the left of the field beyond to another kissing-gate. Cross a small footbridge and then a drive to yet another kissing-gate leading to the playing fields of Baker's Park. Aim for the far right-hand corner and go up some steps and out of the park to a main road.

④ Turn left and after a few yards right into Wolborough Church Path, a surfaced path which emerges after $\frac{1}{4}$ mile or so onto another road, just by Wolborough church. Here you can turn left through a farm gate straight into the field beyond or take a slight detour through the

The River Lemon running through Bradley Wood

churchyard which is an absolute delight, especially in spring when the trees are in blossom. So go through the lychgate and to the right of the church. Take the second path on your left beyond the church up to a gate.

In the field beyond, cross a gravel track to a fingerpost and take the grassy terrace which skirts the hill on the other side (do *not* take the semi-surfaced track half right along the top of the hill). Follow this terrace across the field, with extensive views across to Dartmoor, and follow the hedge on the other side round to the left. Keep following the hedge and path all the way round the hill until you come to another fingerpost.

⑤ Turn left here and go down the hill to a gate into a road. Go right and follow the

> ### PLACES OF INTEREST NEARBY
> The medieval **Bradley Manor,** which you pass along this route, was originally the home of the Bushels, who gave their name to Newton Bushel, one of the two towns that united to form present-day Newton Abbot. It is a National Trust property and is open on Wednesday and Thursday afternoons from April to September. On the other side of Newton Abbot is **Tucker's Maltings,** where barley is malted for the brewing industry. It is open to the public and offers guided tours.

road down to a T-junction; turn right. At the roundabout, go straight on and you will come to the clock tower. Turn left into Bank Street beyond the clock tower, and at the end turn right to return to the pub.

Shaldon
The Ness House Hotel

MAPS: OS LANDRANGER 202 OR EXPLORER 110 (FORMERLY 31) (GR 938719)	**WALK 24**	DISTANCE: $3^3/_4$ MILES

DIRECTIONS TO START: THE A379 COAST ROAD FROM TORQUAY TO TEIGNMOUTH PASSES THROUGH SHALDON. THE NESS HOUSE IS JUST ABOVE THE VILLAGE ON THE TORQUAY SIDE, AND IS SIGNPOSTED FROM THE ROAD. **PARKING:** THE LARGE PUBLIC CAR PARK ALMOST IMMEDIATELY OPPOSITE THE HOTEL.

Shaldon is a delightful village at the mouth of the River Teign, with an attractive foreshore and pretty little lanes running up the hillside behind it. It is particularly popular with the sailing fraternity, and the river is a hive of activity in the summer. The coast along here is particularly spectacular, with sheer red cliffs and long, sandy beaches.

Our route follows the South West Coast Path south from Shaldon, with some superb views along the coast in both directions. We then take a green lane inland, still with excellent views – this time up the river towards Dartmoor – before returning to the hotel along a quiet lane, a riverside path and the side streets of Shaldon.

The Ness House Hotel

This elegant Georgian hostelry is superbly situated at the top of the promontory known as The Ness, with excellent views over Shaldon to the river and Teignmouth. The public accommodation consists of a very comfortable bar and lounge, with settees and armchairs, a beautiful conservatory dining area overlooking the village and the river, and a large garden and patio, also with lovely views. There is also a more formal restaurant, with similar views, serving traditional four-course dinners.

The bar is open all day, and offers a good range of food, from filled baguettes and ploughman's lunches to steaks and specials such as honey-roast pork. On draught you will find Dartmoor Best, plus Tetley's, Castlemaine and Carlsberg Export lagers, Guinness and Inch's Stonehouse cider. Telephone: 01626 873480.

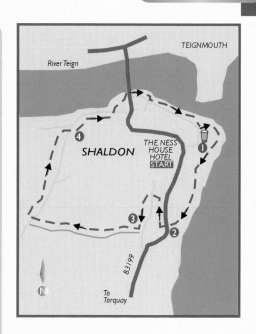

The Walk

① From the hotel garden, take the path that climbs up into Ness Wood. At the top there is a viewpoint from which you can look out over Teignmouth seafront and beach, and along the coast beyond. Follow the path round to the right through the wood along the cliff top and you will eventually come out near the top car park, just above the Shaldon Wildlife Trust. Continue past the car park and follow the path between banks, a little distance from the cliff. About 200 yards beyond the car park, you will find some steps leading up to the left, marked with a yellow waymark.

Climb them and you will emerge at a golf course.

Keep to the left and at the end go through a gap in a hedge. Keep left across the next stretch of the golf course and you will come to a stile. Cross it and go down some steps. There now follows a steep climb up a field. Take it easy and stop at the top for some superb views. At the top the path curves to the right to a stile.

② Cross the stile onto the road beyond and turn right. Go carefully along here, as the road is busy. After 100 yards you will find a public footpath sign on the left; follow it up above the road and through a gate. The path can become a bit overgrown, but it is quite passable. After 75 yards cross a stile and bear left, following the path between two fences. Cross another stile and shortly afterwards turn left, still with fences on either side. The path ends at a stile leading onto a

Shaldon Bridge

lane. Turn left and follow the lane for about ¼ mile until you come to a green lane on the right.

③ Turn along it. As you do so, look to your right for a most attractive view over the River Teign. You continue to catch the view through gateways from time to time, and you also get a very good view up ahead to Dartmoor. When you come to a fork, carry straight on, and at the end of the green lane (some ¾ mile after joining it) you will emerge onto another lane; turn

right. After 500 yards you come to a junction; follow the main lane round to the left. It now descends fairly steeply to a T-junction.

④ Turn right and follow the road as it twists through Ringmore and alongside the river. As the road leaves the riverside you pass a large redstone house with a turret. A short way beyond it, turn left down a little lane to the river again. Follow the riverside path past a children's playground to Shaldon Bridge. Cross the road and continue along a road called Riverside on the other side.

Follow it round to the right, away from the river, and take the second turning on the left, which is signposted to the Potters Mooring Hotel. Pass the bowling green and you will soon find yourself back alongside the river. Follow the riverside road out of the village and up to the right to return to the Ness House Hotel.

PLACES OF INTEREST NEARBY

About 100 yards from the Ness House Hotel, and on the route of the walk, is the **Shaldon Wildlife Trust**, an attractive little zoo which specialises in breeding endangered species. About 5 miles south of Shaldon are the attractions of **Torquay**, including the **Kents Cavern** cave system and the **Babbacombe Model Village**.

Plymouth
The Blackfriars Tavern

MAPS: OS LANDRANGER 201, EXPLORER 108; OR STREET MAP OF PLYMOUTH (GR 481541)	WALK 25	DISTANCE: 2½ MILES

DIRECTIONS TO START: THE PUB IS IN THE BARBICAN, WHICH IS SIGNPOSTED FROM PLYMOUTH CITY CENTRE. IF YOU ARE APPROACHING FROM EXETER, DO *NOT* FOLLOW THE SIGNS FOR THE BARBICAN CAR PARK, BUT CARRY ON TOWARDS THE CITY CENTRE, TURNING OFF LATER, WHERE THERE IS A SIGN TO THE HOE AND THE BARBICAN. **PARKING:** THE ELPHINSTONE OR LAMBHAY HILL CAR PARKS ON THE CLIFF ABOVE THE HARBOUR. THE ROUTE DESCRIPTION STARTS FROM THESE CAR PARKS. (NB: STREET MAPS ARE AVAILABLE FROM THE TOURIST INFORMATION CENTRE IN THE BARBICAN.)

Although Plymouth was heavily bombed during the Second World War and little remains of the original city centre, Sutton Harbour and the historic Barbican area remain largely intact. There is also a great deal to be seen along the Hoe, where Sir Francis Drake famously refused to interrupt his game of bowls just because the Spanish Armada happened to be coming.

This attractive walk explores the narrow, cobbled lanes and Tudor merchants' houses of the Barbican and its surroundings, and then takes you to the Hoe, where you get lovely views over Plymouth Sound. The return leg is along the seafront, passing the imposing Citadel, built by James II in the 17th century as a defence against William of Orange and his supporters.

The Blackfriars Tavern

As the name suggests, this delightful hostelry was once a monastery; indeed, it has only been a pub for a few years. Unusually, it does not open straight onto the street, but is entered through a pretty courtyard. The small bar at the front is sympathetically and tastefully decorated and furnished, and there is a second courtyard through an archway, which is lined with flower-filled tubs and baskets and furnished with tables and chairs. At the back is a restaurant, which is only open in the evenings.

The pub is open all day from 10 am during the summer, but in winter it is closed in the afternoons. The menu ranges from soups, baguettes and jacket potatoes to a good selection of main meals, with the emphasis on seafood. The draught offerings include Guinness and Guinness Extra Cold, Carling, Stella Artois, Worthington Creamflow and Strongbow cider. In the restaurant, one can also get Heineken and Blackthorn cider. Telephone: 01752 254564.

The Walk

① From the Elphinstone car park, turn right into Madeira Road. At the junction, turn right, still in Madeira Road (the road straight on becomes Lambhay Hill). If you have parked in the Lambhay Hill car park, leave by the lower pedestrian exit and turn left into Madeira Road. At the bottom, carry straight on into the Barbican. On your right as you go down, you will see the Mayflower Steps, marking the spot from which the Pilgrim Fathers are believed to have left on their journey to America. Just before the Tourist

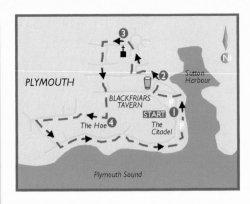

Information Centre turn left into New Street to explore some of the cobbled back lanes. You will pass the Elizabethan House, a lovely Tudor town house, and a little further on the Elizabethan Garden. Both are open to the public. When the cobbled lane ends at a tarred road, turn right down Friar's Lane. At the bottom, turn left into Southside Street, and you will find the Blackfriars Tavern in a courtyard on your left after a few yards.

② To resume the walk continue along Southside Street, and at the end, turn left into Notte Street. After about 100 yards, turn right into St Andrew Street. In the far corner is what is known as the Merchant's House, another 16th-century town house. Follow the street round to the right and after a few yards turn left into Sir John Hawkins Square. At the top

PLACES OF INTEREST NEARBY

There are several interesting buildings one can visit along this route, including the **Elizabethan House** and the **Merchant's House**. The **Plymouth Dome**, on Hoe Road, has a child-friendly exposition of the city's past. And just across Sutton Harbour from the Barbican is the **National Marine Aquarium**.

The statue of Sir Francis Drake on Plymouth Hoe

tarred Promenade running across it.

④ Turn right onto the Promenade. You get a superb view across Plymouth Sound, with Drake's Island just offshore. At the end, join Cliff Road and continue straight on, following the road down a hill. At the T-junction at the bottom, turn left and at the fork, keep to the main street, which is Radford Road. At the next T-junction, turn left into Grand Parade. This becomes Hoe Road, and winds along the edge of the sea. You get another good view across the sound as you follow it, and also the green expanse of the Hoe

of the square turn left and then right into Higher Lane.

③ You pass St Andrew's church on your left, and turn left immediately beyond it, into Royal Parade. Just beyond the church is the Guildhall, which was attractively rebuilt after the Second World War. Turn left just after the Guildhall and pass the courthouse. Cross Princess Street into the tranquil San Sebastian Square. On the other side you go through a pretty garden and cross Notte Street. Carry on up to Citadel Road, and cross that into Hoe Park. This is another lovely park, at the end of which is the Hoe itself, with the

stretching up ahead of you. You pass the Plymouth Dome on your left. Where the road forks, continue along the main route, which is now Madeira Road, as it winds below the 17th century Citadel. It is interesting to note that the guns on this fortress point inland, towards the city, as well as out to sea. James II was as wary of the unruly Plymothians, who were suspected of favouring William of Orange in his struggle for the throne, as he was of William himself! A couple of hundred yards round the corner, you will find the Elphinstone car park on your right, with the Lambhay Hill car park a little further on.

Dartington
The Cott Inn

MAPS: OS LANDRANGER 202 OR OUTDOOR LEISURE 20 (GR 787616)

WALK 26

DISTANCE: 2$\frac{1}{2}$ MILES

DIRECTIONS TO START: DARTINGTON IS AT THE JUNCTION OF THE A384 AND A385 TRUNK ROADS, A MILE OR SO NORTH-WEST OF TOTNES. TO GET TO THE PUB, FOLLOW A NARROW LANE WHICH RUNS SOUTH FROM THE ROUNDABOUT WHERE THE TWO ROADS MEET (SIGNPOSTED TO COTT) FOR $\frac{1}{4}$ MILE. **PARKING:** IN THE PUB CAR PARK (WITH PERMISSION). THERE IS ALSO FREE PARKING AT THE CIDER PRESS CENTRE, ON THE MAIN ROAD (START THE WALK AT POINT 5).

Dartington is the centre of a wide-ranging enterprise which was started in the 1920s by philanthropists Leonard and Dorothy Elmhirst when they bought and restored Dartington Hall, which is now run by a trust. Its activitites include education and the arts (the magnificent 14th century hall is now a college and a centre of the arts), agriculture (the beautiful estate has a large farm) and crafts (the Cider Press Centre sells a wide range of craft items, including the world famous Dartington glass).

This lovely amble takes you through the pretty village of Dartington to the Dartington Hall Estate. There you stroll along a delightful woodland path by a chattering stream before joining the drive up to the hall itself, with good views over the River Dart. The route continues through the hall gardens to the Cider Press Centre.

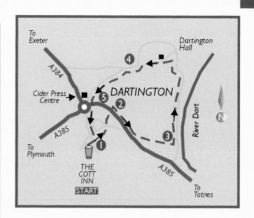

The Cott Inn

This beautiful 14th century inn is a traditional Devon longhouse; when it was still a farmhouse the family would have lived at the upper end of the building, with the livestock at the lower end. It still has the thatched roof, thick cob walls, small windows and low beams associated with that style. Inside, it is divided into two; the upper area constitutes the bar, and is furnished with attractive carved settles and chairs and tables, while the smaller lower end is the restaurant area. There are also tables on the patio outside.

Open all day, the inn offers a wide-ranging buffet at midday, which includes ploughman's lunches as well as hot and cold dishes and sweets; there is an à la carte menu in the evenings. There are usually four cask ales, which change from time to time, as well as John Smith's Extra Smooth, Foster's and Kronenbourg lager, Beamish stout and Strongbow cider. An excellent range of wines is also available. Telephone: 01803 863777.

The Walk

① On leaving the pub go left to the crossroads and turn right (signposted to Staples and Vineyard). Pass a road called Tolchers on your left, and at the next junction turn left. You pass a pretty collection of houses and the lane curves sharply to the left; as it does so, go straight on along a public footpath. This takes you down to the A385. Cross it, taking great care as it is a busy road, and then cross the stone bridge on the other side by an old watermill.

② Turn right and follow the clear path through a wood alongside a stream. You soon veer slightly away from the stream further into the wood, then emerge to find a flood plain – a yellow carpet of buttercups in summer – on your right, with the wood still stretching up the hill on your left. About ¹/₂ mile after you joined it, the path comes out onto the drive to Dartington Hall.

③ Turn left and follow the drive as it climbs gently above the River Dart. Look down to your right for some attractive views over the meadows to the river. After a little more than ¹/₂ mile, take the second turning on the left (signposted 'Deliveries to Hall and White Hart') and you will come to Dartington Hall and its lovely gardens. The buildings are now part of a college and the only part that is open to the public is the Great Hall, and then only when it is not in use. To reach it, go through the gate on your right into the courtyard, and the Great Hall is on your left. You can explore the gardens at will, however. They are always full of interest, but are particularly beautiful in spring and early summer, when the bulbs and many of the shrubs are in flower. To leave the

The Tiltyard at Dartington Hall

gardens, aim for the far right-hand corner, where you will find a gate into a road. (Note: Dogs are not allowed in the gardens; if you have one with you, you will have to continue along the drive and rejoin the route where it emerges from the gate.)

④ Turn left and follow the road for about 300 yards to a junction; turn left (signposted to the Foxhole Centre and the White House Conference Centre). At the next two junctions go straight on, and then go round a gate to reach a road. If you want to visit the main part of the Cider Press Centre, cross over and go down some steps. Otherwise turn left and follow the road round to a smaller complex of shops.

⑤ At the bottom, cross the stream and then a pedestrian crossing across the main road. Go right and then left up a lane. Follow it for $1/4$ mile to the crossroads and the pub.

PLACES OF INTEREST NEARBY

Totnes, about a mile from Dartington, is full of interest. The town centre has been well preserved, and there are some real architectural gems. The Norman castle (English Heritage) is worth a visit, and there is an Elizabethan market on Thursdays.

Cockington
The Drum Inn

MAPS: OS LANDRANGER 202, EXPLORER 110 (FORMERLY 31) OR OUTDOOR LEISURE 20 (GR 894638)

WALK 27

DISTANCE: 2 MILES

DIRECTIONS TO START: COCKINGTON IS BETWEEN TORQUAY AND PAIGNTON AND IS SIGNPOSTED FROM THE SEAFRONT ROAD LINKING THE TWO TOWNS. **PARKING:** THERE IS A PUBLIC CAR PARK OPPOSITE THE PUB.

Cockington is a picturesque village of thatched cottages, most dating back to medieval times, set in a beautiful wooded valley and overlooked by the imposing Cockington Court. The estate has had only three owners since Norman times, and walking through the area is like taking a journey into the past – it is a quiet backwater, a world away from the traffic, the beaches and the amusements of Torbay, even though the seafront is only ³/₄ mile away.

This delightful walk enables you to visit Cockington Court and the attractive little church alongside it before going on to stroll through a wood, shady and cool on hot days, calling at an old gamekeeper's cottage on the way. On the return leg, you take in the gardens around a series of ponds and explore the village centre.

The Drum Inn

There are not many pubs that can boast of having been designed by one of the foremost arrchitects of his era, but the Drum is one. During the 1930s the Cockington Trust commissioned Sir Edwin Lutyens to design a suitable pub for the village.

The result is a roomy, thatched inn with solid beams and wooden posts. There is a large and very attractive garden with a children's play area.

The pub is open all day. It is a Bass house, offering Bass and Fuller's London Pride in the way of real ales. Other beers include Calder's and Tetley's, as well as Carlsberg and Grolsch lagers, Guinness, and Blackthorn if cider is your tipple. There is also a good selection of wines. The menu is extensive, ranging from snacks and main courses to specials such as pork and leek sausages and beef and Stilton pie. Telephone: 01803 690264.

The Walk

① Turn right as you leave the pub and go down some steps to the garden, and then up some more steps on the other side. Go round to the right of the mill pond at the top and then follow the path round to the left and up some more steps. You will come out at the drive to Cockington Court; turn right.

Originally a Tudor manor house, Cockington Court was substantially altered in the 19th century, and most of what one can see today dates from that period. It now houses a pottery and café. Go left when you reach it and you will come to the main door of the lovely little 14th century church.

② Take the path which goes up some steps almost opposite the church door, and at the path junction turn left onto an unsurfaced path. Follow this in amongst trees and rhododendrons. At the fork take the right-hand path, and at the next junction go straight on down some steps. You come out onto some parkland. Turn right onto a grassy path and follow it round to the left and down until it eventually joins a surfaced path which leads off the main drive. (If the various paths seem confusing, don't worry. If you simply keep bearing left you will come out along the drive to Cockington Court, and can rejoin the route at the next point.)

③ Turn right and follow the broad path under a road. At the fork on the other side go right (signposted to woodland walks and the Gamekeeper's Cottage). You will shortly come to the cottage, which dates back to the 16th century. Turn right here (signposted 'woodland walk Warren Barn'). This path takes you along the edge of Manscombe Wood.

④ When the path you are on crosses another, go straight on and after a few yards, just before you reach Warren Barn, turn left, following the public footpath sign. After a hundred yards or so, the

---

PLACES OF INTEREST NEARBY

Cockington is on the outskirts of **Torquay**, with all its attractions, including the **Model Village** at Babbacombe, the network of caves at **Kent's Cavern** and **Bygones**, a reconstruction of a Victorian street.

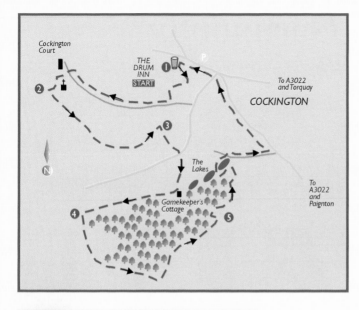

established wood on your left gives way to a stretch of new planting, and then after another 200 yards you go through a gate. Turn left across a stile (signposted 'footpath to Broadley Drive'), still skirting the newly planted area. Cross another stile back into the established growth, and at the end, where another stile leads into a road, turn left to continue round the edge of the wood.

⑤ At the T-junction at the end, turn left again, and after a few yards right; at the fork go right again and down some steps. You emerge onto a surfaced path; you can if you wish turn right to return to the village, but if you turn left a detour of 200-300 yards will take you into the lovely gardens surrounding three ponds (referred to as 'The Lakes', although they are hardly big enough to justify the term). Follow the path around the ponds, which are surrounded by rhododendrons, making a magnificent display in May, and back along the other side. When you reach a drive, turn right and go under an arch beneath the Lower Lodge. You come out at a lane; turn left and follow it into the pretty centre of the village. At the junction bear right and go immediately left through an arch to return to the pub or carry straight on for the car park.

The Gamekeeper's Cottage

Dartmouth
The Cherub Inn

MAPS: OS LANDRANGER 202 OR OUTDOOR LEISURE 20 (GR 877512)

WALK 28

DISTANCE: 4 MILES

DIRECTIONS TO START: FROM TOTNES TAKE THE A381 KINGSBRIDGE ROAD AND TURN OFF ONTO THE A3122. FROM KINGSBRIDGE, TAKE THE A379. THE PUB IS IN HIGHER STREET, IN THE CENTRE OF THE TOWN. **PARKING:** USE THE EXCELLENT PARK-AND-RIDE SERVICE, WHICH OPERATES FROM A CAR PARK ON THE OUTSKIRTS OF TOWN ON THE A3122.

Dartmouth is a lovely, well-preserved town. The River Dart is alive with boats in the summer, and there are narrow streets, steep alleys and secluded courtyards in which you can discover a wealth of hidden architectural delights. And the coast south of the town is magnificent – rugged cliffs and sandy coves backed by rolling hills and farmland.

This route meanders through Dartmouth and then explores the coast and the surrounding countryside. It follows the river to its mouth, past the 14th century Dartmouth Castle, and then swings west along the coast, before heading inland and back to Dartmouth along farm paths and lanes.

The Cherub Inn

This is Dartmouth's oldest house, and dates back to the 14th century. It has a comfortable, cosy bar on the ground floor, with a fireplace at one end, and a beautifully laid out restaurant upstairs. There is a second, overflow restaurant on the second floor.

Visitors are assured of a warm welcome, a good range of ales and a mouthwatering menu. Given their situation, it is hardly surprising that fish features strongly on the menu, but a variety of sandwiches is also offered, as well as soup, steaks and curry. The pub has its own ale (Old Cherub), as well as two or three guest ales. Also on draught are Guinness, Carlsberg and Carlsberg Export, John Smith's and Addlestone's cider. If wine is your drink, there are ten different wines available by the glass. The Cherub is open all day in summer, but closes in the afternoon in winter. Telephone: 01803 832571.

The Walk

①Turn left as you leave the pub and follow Higher Street to the end. Cross Newcomen Road to some steps leading down into Lower Street; turn right. After 100 yards or so you will see the ferry down a lane to your left; go straight on along a narrow lane to a cobbled area alongside the river. Follow this towards Bayard's Cove Fort, built in the 16th century to defend Dartmouth's harbour. Just before the fort, you will find a narrow alley on the right leading up to Castle House Steps; go up here and at the top you will emerge onto a road. Turn left and follow it out of

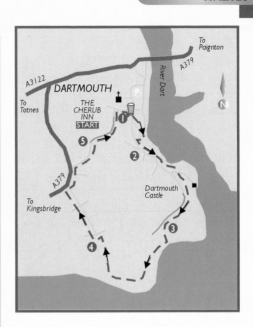

town. You get a good view over the river as you do so.

②Where the road forks go left, keeping to the main road. After 300 yards you come to another fork; go left along Castle Road (signposted to Dartmouth Castle). It takes you round a pretty little cove. At the next junction, go right and then immediately left, following the Coast Path signs. You will now find yourself on a path above the road; when it rejoins the road, go sharp left and then sharp right to visit Dartmouth Castle. Otherwise bear right along the road. After a few yards bear right off the road along a path between banks. This brings you out onto a lane; bear left.

You come to a gateway; at the fork on the other side go left, along the unsurfaced track marked with the Coast Path acorn logo. At the next fork, go right, again following the Coast Path acorn logo. You come out at a surfaced track, and after a few yards there is another fork. Both directions are signposted to Little Dartmouth; take the right-hand one, which gives the distance as 1 mile. You now get a very good view across the Dart estuary. The track leads you to a gate and past some Coastguard cottages to a kissing-gate. Keep to the top of the field beyond, with a magnificent view along the coast.

③ When you get to the next gate, do not go through it, but turn left along the edge of the field and go down to rejoin the Coast Path. Turn right and go through a gate. After about 600 yards you pass a small pond and eventually go through a gate; turn right and another excellent view opens up ahead of you. Keep to the wall on the right. At the end of the wall, go round to the right and follow the fence that replaces it. When you reach a hedge, turn right and go through a kissing-gate. Follow a track along the edge of three fields until you come out through a kissing-gate into a car park.

④ Go through and turn left into a lane; at the junction, follow the main lane round to the right. At the crossroads go straight across, and at the T-junction turn right along the main road. After 100 yards you

> ## PLACES OF INTEREST NEARBY
>
> **Dartmouth Castle**, which you pass along this route, is an English Heritage property and is open to the public. Across the river at Kingswear is the terminus of the **South Devon Railway**, a steam line from Paignton. About 4 miles west of Dartmouth on the A3122 is the **Woodlands Leisure Park**, a popular venue for children.

will see a public footpath sign on the right; cross a stone stile and bear left across a field to another stone stile, which brings you out onto a lane. Turn right and immediately left. After a few yards, at the junction with the main road, turn right and then almost immediately right again down another lane.

⑤ After 500 yards, as the lane turns into a yard, turn right along a surfaced green lane. You descend steeply and as you approach the outskirts of Dartmouth the lane swings left; follow it round and you will emerge onto a residential street. Follow it down to a T-junction and turn right. This street takes you steeply down into the town, winding to the left and the right, and you will soon see Higher Street on your right; turn right and the pub is a few yards along the street.

Noss Mayo
The Ship Inn

MAPS: OS LANDRANGER 201 (START AND FINISH), 202 (MIDDLE) OR OUTDOOR LEISURE 20 (GR 547476)

WALK 29

DISTANCE: 4 MILES

DIRECTIONS TO START: TAKE THE B3186 SOUTH FROM THE A379 PLYMOUTH-KINGSBRIDGE ROAD AT YEALMPTON AND FOLLOW THE SIGNS FOR NOSS MAYO. JUST AFTER YOU PASS THE CHURCH, TURN RIGHT INTO REVELSTOKE ROAD AND AFTER 300 YARDS FOLLOW IT ROUND SHARPLY TO THE RIGHT TO THE VILLAGE CENTRE. **PARKING:** THE PUB CAR PARK IS JUST OFF NOSS HARD. ALTERNATIVELY YOU CAN PARK ON THE HARD ITSELF BUT PLEASE SEE START OF WALK DIRECTIONS.

This picturesque village clings to the hillside above Newton Creek. It has a pleasing mixture of housing, with older fishermen's cottages clustered round the creek and the Hard, and Victorian and modern housing on the slopes above. Together with its bigger neighbour Newton Ferrers, on the other side of the creek, it is a popular haunt for sailors.

The headland south of Noss Mayo was once part of the Revelstoke estate, and this stretch of the South West Coast Path follows a carriage drive constructed by Lord Revelstoke at the end of the 19th century. To reach it, we follow an easy track across a farm, and return to the village along quiet lanes. The coastal views are superb, and thanks to Lord Revelstoke's endeavours they can be enjoyed with the minimum of effort.

The Ship Inn

Situated at the water's edge, this delightful, spacious building dates back to the 16th century. It is set on two floors, with an open staircase connecting them. Tradition has it that there is a smugglers' tunnel from behind the bar to Cellar Beach at the mouth of the Yealm, but it has not been tested! There are log fires in winter, papers to read and a whole wall full of books upstairs.

The pub is open all day from 11.30 am (12 noon on Sundays), and food is available throughout, not just at midday and in the evening. The menu varies from day to day, but typically ranges from sandwiches and grilled baguettes to tempting main courses such as lightly spiced crab cakes, Yealm River moules marinière and roast Devon lamb. Five different real ales are offered, usually local brews, plus Stella Artois, Heineken, Thatcher's Dry cider and Guinness, and a good range of wines. Telephone: 01752 872387.

The Walk

NB: As both these car parks are near the water's edge, it is essential you check the tides. If the tide is in, or you would rather not risk it being in when you return from the walk, it is safer to use the car park higher up the village. Our route passes this on the way from the pub. Instead of following Revelstoke Road when it bends sharp right, go straight on and you will find the car park on your left (see sketch map).

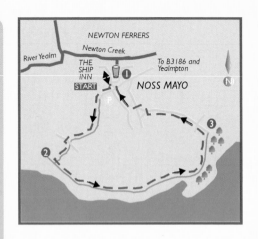

① Turn right if you are leaving via the pub car park, left if you are going direct from the upper floor out into the street. Follow the lane up the hill, and where it turns sharp left, turn right to pass the upper car park and some tennis courts. The lane becomes a track, which climbs up a valley and past a farm. About $1/2$ mile beyond the farm it emerges onto a lane. Turn left and after a few yards right along another track (signposted to the Coast Path). Cross a stile and continue along the track. Cross another stile and make your way down the left-hand side of the field beyond.

② Towards the bottom, you will come to a broad, grassy track; this is Lord Revelstoke's carriage drive; turn left and cross another stile. Follow the track on the other side. You cross another stile and pass Gunrow's Signal Station, a ruined 18th century watch house. After yet another stile you go through a gate. Soon after, you will find a path going right, down towards the sea, signposted to St Peter's church. Do not take it, but keep to the main track as it turns left away from the sea and passes through another gate. After a while the wood opens up and you get another

Blackstone Point, one of the superb views seen on the route

good view along the coast, before entering another stretch of woodland.

③ At the end you go through a kissing-gate into a parking area. Turn left up the lane beyond. At the crossroads about 200 yards further on, go straight across (signposted to Noss Mayo and Newton Ferrers). Follow the lane past the Rowden Court complex and at the junction follow the main lane round to the right (signposted to Noss Mayo and Newton Ferrers again). At the next junction, by the Noss Mayo village sign, do not follow the lane round to the right again, but go straight on through a kissing-gate. Go down alongside a garden and then bear

PLACES OF INTEREST NEARBY
Plymouth is 9 miles away, with a number of attractions, including the **National Marine Aquarium**, the **Dome**, which has displays of Plymouth's history, and the historic **Barbican** area.

right into a wood, descending quite steeply. At the bottom, go through another kissing-gate and down some steps into a lane; turn right. At the T-junction turn right (or left to return to the upper car park) and immediately left down the hill. At the bottom you will find the Hard on your right and the pub beyond.

Bantham
The Sloop Inn

MAPS: OS LANDRANGER 202 OR OUTDOOR LEISURE 20 (GR 669436)

WALK 30

DISTANCE: 3 MILES

DIRECTIONS TO START: TURN SOUTH-WEST OFF THE A379 PLYMOUTH-KINGSBRIDGE ROAD BETWEEN AVETON GIFFORD AND CHURCHSTOW, FOLLOWING THE SIGNS FOR BANTHAM. **PARKING:** IN THE LARGE PUBLIC CAR PARK BY THE BEACH, ABOUT 200 YARDS BEYOND THE PUB.

The South Hams, the area south and west of Totnes, is one of the most beautiful corners of Devon. It is a region of rich farmland, miles of breathtaking coastline and some of the most picturesque villages in the county – and this walk gives you a taste of all three.

It starts in Bantham, a pretty little village at the mouth of the Avon River,

with an extensive golden beach beyond it. We then take farm paths and tracks over the downs to Bantham's larger neighbour Thurlestone, where we join the South West Coast Path. The return leg follows this path along the clifftop, with magnificent views of the coast in both directions. Apart from one stiff but mercifully short climb near the start, it is a very easy but very rewarding walk.

The Sloop Inn

This 16th century hostelry comprises one large L-shaped room, the front part of which has a slate floor, while the rest is tastefully carpeted and furnished with comfortable chairs and benches. Wooden panelling gives it a warm, cosy atmosphere and the staff are friendly and welcoming. There is a paved area at the back if you want to enjoy a meal in the sun, and a log stove to keep you warm in winter.

The menu is extensive, and includes fresh fish and shellfish, vegetarian and meat dishes, as well as soups and snacks. Fresh local produce is used wherever possible. There is a good wine list, and several ales are offered – Bass, their own Sloop Inn Ale and Palmer's at the time of writing. Also on tap are Boddingtons, Heineken, Stella Artois and Foster's lagers, Guinness and the local Luscombe cider. The pub is open at the usual times midday and evening, but closed during the afternoon. Telephone: 01548 560489.

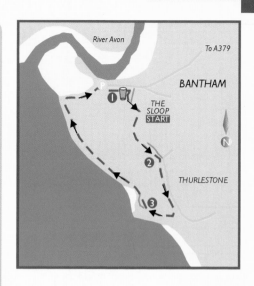

The Walk

① As you leave the pub turn right and then immediately right again. You pass some holiday flats and follow a track on the other side. Where the track ends go straight on over a stile onto a path between hedges. Cross another stile at the end and go diagonally left across the field beyond to a third stile. Cross a small field beyond to yet another stile, and on the other side go right and then left to climb a short but steep hill. As you climb, you get a good view on your right down the valley to the sea.

At the top, you climb some steps and cross another stile. Carry on across another field, and keep to the right of the one beyond. In the next field, follow the clear path which takes you slightly away from the right-hand boundary. Cross yet another stile (your eighth if you are counting) and keep to the left of the next field to a stone stile. This takes you onto a track, which leads down to the green at Thurlestone.

② Here you meet a road; bear right and follow the road out of the village, past some tennis courts and a golf course. The flowers in the hedgerows along here are lovely in summer. You will see a footpath sign pointing right across the golf course; ignore it and carry straight on. About 100 yards beyond the clubhouse, you will see another footpath sign pointing right to the beach; take that. Cross a stile and a field to a path between hedges. This brings you out at a lane running alongside a beach; you are now on the South West Coast Path.

Bantham beach

③ Turn right, and after a few yards go left, leaving the lane, to follow a path above the beach. At the edge of the golf course, turn left, following the Coast Path sign. The path now winds for about $1^{1}/_{4}$ miles between the golf course and the cliff. Along this stretch you get an excellent view back down the coast. As you round Warren Point, you get another superb view ahead of you. Once again, the flowers make a beautiful show here in spring and summer.

At the end of the golf course, cross a stile and continue along the Coast Path as it goes down a field and curves round the headland known as The Ham. You get another lovely view over Bantham beach, and also across to Burgh Island. As you go along the bottom of the field you will come to a gate and stile on your left; cross the stile and follow a track to the beach car park. To return to the Sloop, cross the car park and follow the lane beyond into the village.

PLACES OF INTEREST NEARBY

Just north of Kingsbridge, about 6 miles from Bantham, is the **Sorley Tunnel Adventure Farm**, a farm park and craft centre. And just outside Salcombe, about 10 miles away, is the National Trust property of **Overbecks House**, which has a magnificent clifftop garden.